D0918142

HAUNTED RAILS

About the Author

Matthew L. Swayne (State College, PA) is a journalist who currently works as a research writer at Penn State. He is also the author of *Haunted World War II* and *Haunted Rock and Roll.* Matt has worked as a reporter and music reviewer for several newspapers and online outlets. He has been a featured guest on several podcasts and radio shows, including *Coast to Coast AM* and *The Darkness.*

MATTHEW L. SWAYNE

HAUNTED RAILS

Tales of Ghost Trains, Phantom Conductors, and Other Railroad Spirits

Llewellyn Publications
Woodbury, Minnesota

FIRST EDITION
First Printing, 2019

Cover design by Shannon McKuhen
Interior photographs are courtesy of the Library of Congress Prints and Photographs Division.

Library of Congress Cataloging-in-Publication Data
Names: Swayne, Matthew L., author.
Title: Haunted rails : tales of ghost trains, phantom conductors, and other railroad spirits / by Matthew L. Swayne.
Description: First edition. | Woodbury, MN : Llewellyn Publications, [2019] | Includes bibliographical references.
Identifiers: LCCN 2019016662 (print) | LCCN 2019981104 (ebook) | ISBN 9780738761336 (alk. paper) | ISBN 9780738761510 (ebook)
Subjects: LCSH: Ghosts. | Haunted places. | Railroads—Miscellanea.
Classification: LCC BF1461 ,S928 2019 (print) | LCC BF1461 (ebook) | DDC 133.1/22—dc23
LC record available at https://lccn.loc.gov/2019016662
LC ebook record available at https://lccn.loc.gov/2019981104

Llewellyn Publications
A Division of Llewellyn Worldwide Ltd.
2143 Wooddale Drive
Woodbury, MN 55125-2989
www.llewellyn.com

Printed in the United States of America

Other Books by Matthew L. Swayne

Haunted Valley: The Ghosts of Penn State

America's Haunted Universities

Haunted Rock and Roll

More Haunted Rock and Roll

Ghosts of Country Music

Haunted World War II

Dedication

I come from a long line of railroaders. My grandfather and his father worked, in different parts of their careers, as firemen and engineers for the Pennsylvania Railroad and for the later railroad companies that emerged from PRR. This book is dedicated to my grandfather, Bernard Bookhamer, a lifelong railroader whose stories inspired my interest in trains and railroad history.

This book is also dedicated to my grand-niece Layla Smith and bananas.

Contents

A Note of Caution xv

Introduction 1

Chapter 1: Ghost Trains, Haunted Engines, and Haunted Cabooses 5

Abraham Lincoln Ghost Train 6

Ghostlore or Something More? 9

Any Evidence of a True Haunting? 11

Rebel Ghost Train Rises Again 12

Bravehaunts: The Ghost Trains of Scotland 16

Terror on the Tay Bridge 16

Gorbals Ghost Train 17

Demon Train 18

A Time-Traveling Ghost Train? 19

Ghost Train of the Santa Ana 20

What's Behind the Haunting? 22

Do Famous Sci-Fi Writers Dream of Locomotive Spirits? 23

Ghost Train or Eerie Railroad Premonition? 26

Scary Scandinavian Ghost Train 29

Chapter 2: Haunted Cabooses 33

Possessed Caboose 34

Haunted Caboose, Female Ghost 37

Haunted Caboose Hotels 40

Featherbed Inn 41

The Canyon Motel 43

Chapter 3: Haunted Railroad Museums 45

The Railroaders Memorial Museum 46

Investigation at the Museum 47

Famous—or Infamous—Frank 50

Why Frank? 51

More Haunted Happenings 52

So Why Is the Museum Haunted? 53

Has a Haunted Hobo Boarded a Railroad Museum Without a Pass? 54

Waves of Paranormal Phenomena 57

Of History, Heritage, and Hauntings 60

Going Deeper 63

Railroad Ghosts or Not? 63

National Railroad Museum Features a Five-Star Haunting 64

Locked In 66

Georgia State Railroad Museum 67

Red Coat 69

Paranormal Check 69

Blacksmith Shop Haunts 70

Print Shop 70

Skeptics and Believers 71

Restless Spirits in the Sleeping Quarters 71

Chapter 4: Haunted Stations 75

Was a Weird Specter Seen at a Train Yard Sent to Warn Workers, Residents? 77

Civil War Spirits Haunt Gettysburg Engine House 81

Tracking Ogden's Historic Railroad Past and Its Haunted Present 84
An Ongoing Investigation 85
Yahudi 86
Why So Haunted? 87
Bloody Luggage 88
Ogden Exchange Building 89
Ghosts on the Waterfront 91
I'll Come Back Another Time 94
Groups of Ghosts 94
Tubes of Terror: The UK's Supernatural Subway System 95
South Kensington Station 96
Bethnal Green 97
Liverpool Street Station 98
Becontree Station 100
Union Station and the Ghost of Abigail 101
First-Hand Account 104

Chapter 5: Haunted Tunnels.................................. 107
The Haunted Horseshoe Curve 108
Tunnel of Terror—Sensabaugh Tunnel's Dark Past May Shed Light on Its Current Paranormal Popularity 111
Flinderation and the Supernatural Railroad Nation 114
"Pushing Out of the Way" 116
Other Spectral Suspects 117

Chapter 6: Haunted Tracks and Accident Sites 119
Eerie Echoes—The Return of the Red Arrow 120
Dead Railroad Men Do Tell Tales 122
Bodies Exhumed, Spirits Remain 125
The Legends of America's Most Haunted Railroad Crossing 126
Historic Evidence? 130
Spirit Photography Captures Eerie Signs of Haunted Railroad History 131
What's Behind the Haunting? 132
Other Witnesses 134
The Case of the Chatsworth Disaster and the Glowing Grave 136
The Screaming Bridge 140

Chapter 7: Haunted Railroad People: Engineers, Conductors, Brakemen, Workers, and Accident Victims 145
Railroad Ghost Story Gets Presidential Seal of Approval 146
Natural Explanations? 149
Disappearing Lights 151
The Paulding Light 151
Skeptics Respond 153
A Spectral Brakeman Who Never Takes a Break 154
1888 Ghost Rider of the Rails 156
A Not-So-Thankful Thanksgiving Day Haunting 158
Truth or Folklore? 160

He May Have Died at His Station but He Left a Restless Spirit 161
The Natural State Boasts Some Supernatural Railroad Tales 164
Money, Murder, and Mysterious Lights 164
The Beheaded Brakeman of Crossett 166
Northern Spook Light: Canada's Famous Railway Ghost Light 167
Phenomenon Debunked? 168
The Suitor House: Canada's Spirit Weigh Station 170
Dead Worker's Ghost Gives Whole New Meaning to Being "Fired" 172

Conclusion: Travelogue for a Trip on the Haunted Rails 177

Notes and Sources 183

A NOTE OF CAUTION

Before you delve into the spooky railroad stories and ghostlore, I would like to add this bit of caution. Railroading is a dangerous business. In my opinion, one of the reasons ghost stories arise from railroad history so frequently in the first place is because it's so darn dangerous. Accidents have maimed and killed thousands of railroad workers and passengers over the years. You may be tempted to explore some of these railroad spirits on your own. Don't. While researching this book, I came across at least one account of a ghost hunter being killed while conducting an investigation of a haunted railroad site. You don't have to be worried about the ghosts scaring you; there's enough real danger out there.

Beyond that, railroad property is often private, and you can get arrested or fined for trespassing.

There are plenty of ways to safely and legally research railroad ghosts. Railroad museums hold ghost hunts, and some are even open to allowing paranormal investigation teams to come in on off-hours to find evidence. Some abandoned railroad sites are now part of rails-to-trails projects and offer a much safer environment for finding out whether ghosts really do haunt the tracks and trains.

So be safe and be smart if you decide to investigate the connection between the paranormal and railroad history.

INTRODUCTION

When I was young, I would lie in bed and listen to the non-stop train traffic as the engines curled around the big bend that arched along the Little Juniata River, a stream that meandered just a couple hundred yards from my family's house in Tyrone, Pennsylvania. Like a ghost that rattles its chains or screams in the night, the train could often be heard long before there was any visible manifestation. First, the engine's banshee horn moaned—part warning, part celebration—as it neared the station a few miles away, then the throaty diesel engine roared as it got closer, the percussive ensemble of steel wheels slapped along steel tracks and, finally, the rhythmic stomp of cars rocked along the rails.

At night, if I looked out the window, I could see a train headlamp scanning the path ahead, like a lost soul.

And, moments later, it was all gone. Vanished.

The whole encounter seemed ghostly to me.

Railroads, too, haunted the past of my community. The sounds of trains that came through town continually gave me a sense of comfort. These machines and the people who worked on them—people like my grandfather and dozens of others in my town—were delivering fuel and food, and who knows what else. They carried travelers home to loved ones waiting just beyond the horizon, where the rusty parallel tracks merged into one. When the railroad reigned as king in central Pennsylvania, the industry also invested heavily in the communities and in the workers and their families. The companies built bridges and developed infrastructure, constructed massive factories and roundhouses, and carved paths through the limestone-studded mountains. For the workers, these companies didn't just provide jobs. They also built parks and recreation facilities for the workers and their families.

As the rail industry became less profitable and, therefore, less important, and as freight and passenger money switched more often to cars and trucks, these giant companies—the Pennsylvania Railroad and Conrail, for example—faded, too, taking away jobs and that precious community support.

But evidence still remains of the central role the railroad played in the region. Some of the old buildings remain. They're vacant and idle, but the facades and shells are visible. A few station houses and other railroad outbuildings still stand. Several bridges are intact. And trains continue to run—bound for glory—through the hills and across the fields.

But that's not the only reminder that's left of the once-dominant railroad industry. There are ghost stories. Lots of them.

In *Haunted Rails*, you'll find many tales of ghost trains that glide silently through the countryside along long, unused stretches of rails, legends of engineers and crew members who perished in tragic crashes but continue to haunt railroad landmarks, and stories about railroad workers who still show up for work years after their deaths. These are some of the most common motifs in a subsection of haunted mythology and folklore—often referred to as ghostlore.

Some of the stories I collected for this book can't quite be classified as ghostlore because the people who tell the tales are real people who claim they have had real encounters with some of these railroad spirits. I usually dub these stories "ghost accounts" or "paranormal encounters."

There are some stories that combine both the elements of ghostlore and paranormal encounters to create a genre all their own. In one case, a town's railroad ghostlore led to the discovery of an actual mass grave and, possibly, evidence of a mass murder.

All these stories are covered here, and you can decide whether the accounts are real ghost stories, made-up mythology, or, quite possibly, something in between.

Check your itinerary. It looks like your first stop is a visit to places where ghost trains are rumored to still ride the rails and spirits are said to lurk in railroad cars and cabooses. That's all ahead in the first chapter: Ghost Trains, Haunted Engines, and Haunted Cabooses.

All aboard!

—— Chapter 1 ——

GHOST TRAINS, HAUNTED ENGINES, AND HAUNTED CABOOSES

In this chapter, we will delve into a unique piece of railroad ghostlore: the ghost train. This requires some explaining. We're accustomed to the notion of a haunted house, but what about haunted trains? These are trains that supposedly attract the ghostly interactions of spirits, entities, poltergeists, and any of the other cast of characters listed in the paranormal panoply.

But ghost trains are different: the apparition is the entire train.

In this chapter, there are examples of macabre ghost trains and ones that are mostly untethered from any human engineer or railroad crew.

Next, though, we patiently wait along the tracks on a pitch-black April night for a ghost train that some say appears each year—a grim reminder of a funeral train that rose from the ashes of a divided nation and animated by the spirit of an assassinated president.

Abraham Lincoln Ghost Train

Illinois

We'll start our journey aboard one of the oldest, and certainly the most famous ghost trains: the Abraham Lincoln funeral train.

As the winds of the Civil War blew across the country, United States military officials ordered the construction of a train that would be used expressly for President Abraham Lincoln. The military thought the President could use the train not just as a means of transportation but as a symbolic way to unify the country once the war was over. The train would lead a grand victory tour of the country, or so they thought.

The military even briefed Lincoln on the train tour. But the president, somewhat strangely, wanted no part of the idea. On the surface, Lincoln's argument against a presidential train was simple: it cost too much. But aides wondered if something else bugged Lincoln, a man known for his deep intuitive, and some would suggest, psychic powers. They just couldn't figure out why Lincoln protested so vehemently against the presidential train proposal.

Despite Lincoln's protest, there would be a presidential train, which would be named the Old Nashville. In fact, some sources indicate the president finally arranged an official visit and tour of the train. His tour was scheduled for April 15, 1865, the day he was assassinated.

Sadly, instead of a grand victory tour, the train pulled the Great Emancipator on a grand tour into the afterlife. On that drizzly morning of April 19, 1865, the weather matched the mood of the nation. Approximately 10,000 people gathered to watch Lincoln's legendary funeral train depart from the depot in Washington, DC, on a circuitous journey to Springfield, Illinois. Draped in dark garlands, the nine-car train passed through more than 400 communities during the journey, traveling through the main stops of Baltimore, Maryland; Harrisburg, Pennsylvania; Philadelphia, Pennsylvania; New York City; Albany, New York; Buffalo, New York; Cleveland, Ohio; Columbus, Ohio; Indianapolis, Indiana; Michigan City, Indiana; and Chicago, Illinois, before arriving at the president's final resting place in Springfield, Illinois, on May 3, 1865. Officials picked the route to reverse Lincoln's inauguration journey to the White House.

This train car carried the body of President Abraham Lincoln to his final resting place in Illinois.

Paranormal theorists suggest that the trauma the nation suffered during Lincoln's assassination ensured that this funeral train could never truly reach its final destination, and that it must continue to retrace that somber route on the anniversary of the event for eternity.

Some people who are brave enough, or crazy enough, to wander near the railroad lines that were once part of the funeral train's original itinerary say a strange feeling has served as a premonition that something is about to happen. They say it feels like time is standing still. Literally. The hands of their watches don't seem to move and the numbers of digital time-keeping devices never advance.

If it's a clear night, witnesses say clouds drift over the moon to make the night pitch black.

Then, the sounds of a train—the grinding steel wheels and the sizzling of steam—echo across the dark night sky. A blinding glare of an engine's spotlight appears on the horizon and the rest of the train slowly emerges. Witnesses who see the train say it's a near-exact likeness of the pictures of the funeral train published in history books and seen on video documentaries about the event. But there are a few differences. For example, some claim that the train belches huge explosions of fire, not listed as one of the options on the president's official mortal locomotive.

As the spectral train passes, witnesses see that it's not just a ghost train: it's a ghost train filled with ghosts. People report that through the train windows they can see a coffin laid out, covered in an American flag. Watching over the coffin are a squad of silent, stoic men, who are the spirits of dead Union soldiers that must guard the body of the president for eternity.

Witnesses say that after the train passes, watches or timepieces restart, but have usually lost about eight minutes.

Ghostlore or Something More?

It sounds like a great piece of American ghostlore, which is just folklore and legends that center on spirits. But has anyone actually seen, or even thought they've seen the Lincoln funeral train for real? The answer is: maybe.

While all kinds of ghost hunting evidence, such as electronic voice phenomena (EVP) and photographic anomalies, have been collected about haunted railroad phenomena throughout the world, that type of hard evidence is especially difficult to find about the Abraham Lincoln funeral ghost train.

A few personal accounts do exist from people who purport to have a run-in with the funeral ghost train. An anonymous account found on the *Seeking Ghosts* blog suggests that some of these paranormal buffs have captured more than just folklore. The details of this story read like much of the folklore collected about the funeral train, but it starts—unlike the legend—in a car at a railroad crossing near a depot. According to the writer, he was stopped at the depot on an exceptionally dark night. He saw two railroad workers chatting on the train platform. Besides him and the workers, there was no one else around.

As he lifted his foot from the brake and began to press on the gas pedal, the arms of the railroad crossing gate fell and its lights began to flash. Then an odd train whistle shrieked, but it sounded different from the usual diesel-powered trains that frequently travel through the town. In fact, the approaching train looked completely different from the modern trains the writer frequently saw. This was an old-fashioned steam engine. Even more bizarre, the train tugged several antique cars, all draped in black crepe, he wrote. He also noticed that the train didn't make a sound as it chugged toward him.

As he watched the engine pull into the depot, a blue glow surrounded the entire length of the train. It stopped briefly at the depot. The train slowed and stopped at the depot platform. The whistle blew once more. As the locomotive drew closer, the anonymous witness said he had a chance to take a much closer look, maybe too close of a look.

"One train car that stopped directly in front of me was decked out even more ornately," he wrote. "I saw through its large windows a coffin. It dawned on me that this must be a funeral coach. An honor guard of soldiers watched over the casket inside. When I looked closer, I was taken aback, for these soldiers appeared to be skeletons."

He even wrote that he saw a band on the train—a skeleton band, to be exact.

"To the side of this car a band of soldiers played slowly what I assumed was a dirge," the writer added. "They, too, were skeletons dressed in midnight blue uniforms. I realized that I heard no music."

The train disappeared into the night just as silently and frightfully as it had appeared. Before it completely vanished, a final echo of the phantom whistle pealed into the night.

Entranced by the spectral and skeletal spectacle, the writer suddenly remembered the workers on the platform, who remained frozen like statues as the train passed. Probably scared stiff. But at least there were other witnesses, he thought.

He said he left his car to talk to the men.

"My legs shaking, I got out of my car and walked to where the other two men stood. When I questioned them, they told me that no train was scheduled to travel through town that night."

And now we are left with this question: Is this just a good piece of fiction writing, or is there something more going on along the path of American history's saddest train trip?

Any Evidence of a True Haunting?

Accounts of actual encounters with the funeral ghost train, like the one discussed above, are fairly standard and similar. A quick web search will bring up a few. Newspapers also have a few articles, some stretching back decades, about visits from the funeral ghost train.

However, it's hard to find accounts of any witnesses who will sign their name to it.

When in doubt, I usually rely on paranormal investigation teams to provide some actual evidence of any real encounter with the Abraham Lincoln funeral ghost train. Maybe a train horn caught using electronic voice phenomenon equipment? An image of a ghost train snapped by a digital camera?

Unfortunately, I came up empty here as well. In fact, I haven't been able to track down a paranormal team that investigated the annual visit of the funeral train, let alone any evidence they might have collected.

And that's okay.

Ghostlore is an important way to connect with history. Each time you tell a ghost story, or repeat a bit of ghostlore, you're helping to pass on, in a way, a history lesson. The story of Lincoln's train is a great case study. The story reminds us on a yearly basis of the great man's accomplishments, as well as his sacrifices.

Still, if you're stopped at a railroad crossing some midnight in April and your watch suddenly stops as a steam engine carrying skeleton soldiers and band members crosses in front of you, make sure you send me a note, or an email.

Rebel Ghost Train Rises Again

West Point, Virginia

Historians consider Confederate General Thomas "Stonewall" Jackson one of the early masters of incorporating the railroad into actual military campaigns. In his brilliant Shenandoah campaign in 1862, Jackson used the near-magical speed of trains to help deceive his Union enemy. In one bold move, Jackson marched his army out of the Shenandoah Valley toward Richmond, Virginia, leaving his Union counterparts to conclude Jackson's troops were retreating, or were responding to orders to reinforce the Confederate capital. Once out of sight, though, the Confederates hopped a ride on a train and stealthily arrived back in the valley, where Jackson launched a violent surprise attack on Union armies, sending them into a disorganized retreat.

But Jackson wasn't the only one who recognized the strategic and tactical military advantage of the railroad. In fact, you might say that the military capacity and value of the railroad came of age during the Civil War. It also made trains, railroad factories, and the rail lines themselves tempting targets of rampaging raiders and cavalry units.

That might explain the following story from the Tidewater region of Virginia.

For years, residents of nearby West Point, Virginia, have claimed they have seen strange lights hovering just down the tracks from a railroad crossing located on Route 30. One of the explanations for the ghost lights goes back to the Civil War. According to the tale, a train full of wounded Confederate soldiers who were urgently needed for a looming battle never arrived at its destination. When rescuers rode up the line to see what had happened, thinking perhaps the train had broken down, the mystery only deepened. There were no signs of either the train, or its passengers. The train had seemingly disappeared.

But trains don't just disappear. People quickly guessed at what had happened: Union raiders stumbled onto the train and attacked; they killed all the soldiers on board and then burned the train. Another guess: the Union soldiers stole the train.

Whatever had happened, there are those who believe the lights that play along the train tracks are evidence that the train is gone, but that the ghost train will live forever. People still claim it's now a ghost train that continues to roll down the spectral tracks near West Point. Some people see the lights of an old-fashioned steam train and hear its phantom bell and whistle.

Like all good railroad spook stories, though, this tale features some clever historical revisionism mixed in with some actual weird phenomena. People really do spot strange lights and orbs at the crossing.

For instance, a few members of the West Point Historical Society told the *Virginia Gazette* that they've witnessed the lights. The description of those lights—the color, how high off the ground, and the number—varies from witness to witness. Member Edwin Malechek told the paper he first saw the lights back in the 1960s when he and his friends were out for a summer adventure. Malechek, along with his friends, saw something that looked "like a big flashlight" swaying back and forth. He said it was spotted on the eastern side of the crossing beyond the tree line.

Another member of the historical society, Donald O'Connor, said he had his own brush with haunted Civil War rails. O'Connor, also of the historical society, said he and his group of high school friends saw the light a few times. When he and his buddies saw the light, which he described as fuzzy and round, they claimed it hovered just above the train tracks. He told the newspaper he saw the light on two occasions.

One witness told a more graphic tale in an email sent to *Haunted VA Blogspot*, a website that focuses on Virginia-area hauntings. He said a whole bunch of witnesses got a good look at the light when it appeared.

"Everyone gasped in shock at the exact same moment, which tells me it wasn't any kind of figment or our eyes playing tricks on us," he wrote.

They thought it might be some local trickster but then discounted that: the area is remote and there were no signs of other vehicles.

The writer continued: "It looked like a welding arc. It was bright and shimmered for about three or four seconds and vanished. It appeared very far away. The second time it appeared as red, moving from left to right and it illuminated the tops of the rails, so it was easy to gauge its distance. The light appeared to turn into several lights and they again vanished after about four seconds. It then appeared randomly four more times, each time moving closer to our location. The last two appearances were in quick succession about ten seconds apart and they very clearly illuminated the ground underneath."

Based on all the testimonies from witnesses that stretch back over decades, it's hard to discount that *something* is happening on those Tidewaters tracks, but not everyone buys the Civil War ghost train story.

First, there's no historical record of Confederate trains disappearing there.

Local historian Bill Palmer told the *Virginia Gazette* that the way the story portrays the Union attack in the area is problematic. Confederates had stopped Union forces outside of Richmond. If the Confederates had decided to evacuate the wounded by train, they would have moved them away from the fighting to Richmond, not to West Point, Palmer added.

Palmer pointed out another anomaly. According to his research, the lights started to appear in the 1950s. "If they were Confederate ghosts, they waited almost 100 years before doing ghostly things," he told the paper.

Still, he does admit that this section of rail, like a lot of tracks, has its share of tragedies. A train derailed in the 1880s, but no deaths were reported, and a mother and daughter died in a vehicle-locomotive accident in the 1950s.

And that might lead some ghost light believers to conjecture: If the lights started to appear in the 1950s, could the spook lights be related to this accident?

To that skeptics might add: Or does that just mean that the spook lights are nothing more than headlights?

The debate on the Confederate ghost train—like the ghosts of Civil War heroes and the spirits of restless train engineers—seem to be eternal.

Bravehaunts: The Ghost Trains of Scotland

Scotland

There's something solemnly spooky about Scotland. Misty and majestic, the United Kingdom's rugged northern land rightly takes its place as arguably the kingdom's most haunted. And if ghosts do traverse the moors and mountains of Scotland, they probably take the train.

Scotland is the home to several tales about ghost trains that scream through the night. Some are related to incidents of the country's railroad past. The origin of other stories is a little harder to nail down.

We'll start with a disastrous train wreck, the echoes of which, apparently, are still resounding across the dark, moody waves.

Terror on the Tay Bridge

The Tay Bridge spans the Firth of Tay between Wormit and Dundee. In the late nineteenth century, the bridge, designed by Sir Thomas Bouch, stood as a testament to man's ingenuity. Bouch received a knighthood from Queen Victoria, in part because of this achievement. But Mother Nature has an ingenuity all her own, and a destructive follow-through to match. On a December evening in 1879, a storm battered the bridge with side winds, causing a section of the mighty structure to tumble into the waves like it was made of matchsticks.

A train crossing the bridge plummeted into the water, killing all—at least 75—on board. But one more name would be added to that list. Bouch's design never accounted for wind load. That, and other design problems, were blamed for the disaster. The engineer died within a year.

Since then, witnesses say that on the anniversary of the disaster, a ghost train crosses the Firth where the bridge once stood. More hauntedly, they say you can hear the screams.

Paranormal investigator Geoff Holder, author of *Haunted Dundee*, decided to spend the evening of the anniversary near the site of the collapse. He reported nothing strange happened that night—no screams and no apparitions of six-carriage trains appearing in mid-air.

But that hasn't stopped some believers from continuing to tell the tale. After all, the Tay Bridge Train of Terror is just one of many ghost trains tied to the sites of railroad disasters.

Gorbals Ghost Train

Gorbals is a section of Glasgow that sits on the south bank of the river Clyde. It became a center of the city's rapid industrialization, and steam-powered locomotives played a huge role in that.

This mixture of steam-powered and spirit-drenched Scotland produced an unforgettable encounter for Tom Rannachan, a psychic medium who writes about it in *Psychic Scotland*. According to Rannachan, as a child, he and a group of friends and family decided to investigate a claim that a ghost train still rode the rails of an abandoned section of track in Gorbals. In the evening, they climbed through nettles and up an embankment to reach the site. And it was nothing to look at—just a bunch of rusty rails.

The band of little ghost hunters stayed silent until someone shouted, "There's a ghost train coming!" Rannachan can't remember hearing or seeing anything out of the ordinary at that moment; he was too busy running. But when he reached their entry point he looked back.

"I swear there was this huge, dark steam train making its way along the tracks toward us," he wrote. "I remember the whole scene as if it was yesterday; the smoke and the sound as the ghastly locomotive travelled along the broken tracks."

But, Rannachan knows there's a problem with his testimony. He's a psychic. Maybe he just saw the whole thing through his mediumistic powers.

Rannachan wrote that he asked his cousin, who had accompanied him on the ghost train hunt, and she not only remembered the night in question but actually remembered the ghost train.

The psychic chalks up the adventure as just another night in the life of a psychic medium in Scotland, a place he calls "one of the most spiritually rich places on earth."

Demon Train

Another source of railroad hauntings are accidents and crimes, and they prompt their share of ghosts. Strong personalities—railroad workers who just won't die, for example—are another reason for railroad hauntings. Scotland has a unique Celtic twist to a tale of a spooky railroad legend. Celtic mythology suggests that nature spirits inhabit the earth, the water, and the skies of the region we now refer to as the United Kingdom.

These spirits, natives say, must be appeased, or, at the very least, respected. The coming of the steam engine at the advent of the Industrial Age neither respected, nor made any attempt to appease, native spirits. And those spirits took their revenge.

In the Scottish Highlands, residents near the Kyle of Lochalsh say that when railroad engineers built a rail line through the countryside, the native spirits were angered. Their revenge: a ghost train. People said they've seen an ominous-looking black locomotive racing along the tracks. It doesn't just send smoke and steam billowing into the air. Witnesses say it also shoots out flames.

They add that the train heads directly into those sacred Scottish hills.

And disappears.

A Time-Traveling Ghost Train?

South Wales

Two Welsh fishermen took a few moments to load up their tackle and gear and head home after another successful day on the stream. Although it's unclear how many fish they caught, it was successful because, as the old saying goes, *even a bad day fishing is better than your best day at work.*

The men were fishing along a pristine stretch of one of the United Kingdom's best trout streams. In the 1860s, this parcel was considered one of the finest spots for fishing because the Industrial Revolution, which was paving the rest of Europe, had happened to leave this spot of wilderness virtually untouched.

But the Industrial Revolution was about to make a loud, and spooky, introduction—or maybe it was about ready to make a loud premonition.

One of the men—who owned a nearby farm—was enjoying a little extra time on the river and lingered a bit longer than his friend. He later said that as he paused and lit his pipe, he felt the earth tremble slightly, or maybe it wasn't trembling at all. It was, as he described it, a peculiar sensation. Everything was silent around him, but full of noise, he tried to explain. That tremble eventually erupted. It knocked the pipe out of his hand. Briefly, he thought about running away, but a shrill whistle froze him in place. He said he heard what could only be described as the grinding of thousands of wheels. He watched as a herd of horses reared up and ran—scared out of their wits—away from the noise and toward the stream.

Eventually, the terrible noise faded away, leaving the poor fisherman all alone with an incredible mix of fear and wonderment. What was the noise? What did he experience?

Those questions may have been answered years later when engineers tore a hole in the mountains near that spot to make way for the South Wales Railway.

The reporter wrote about the opening of that tunnel in the paper, *Once A Week*, saying, "The mouth of which opened at the very spot from whence what was now explained as a spectral train had issued, and upon opening day the farmer and a crowd of country folk upon the spot to witness the effect, which certainly exactly answered the description by him, even to the horses galloping into the Tav."

Other elders of the towns surrounding the new railway claimed that they, too, saw a ghost train roaring across the valley long before the railroad was built.

Was it a premonition? Was it a time slip? Or was it another example of spectral trains?

Those questions remain unanswered.

Ghost Train of the Santa Ana

Santa Ana, California

Trains once chugged along the line that ran northwest from Santa Ana, California, to Anaheim. Built in the late 1870s to early 1880s, the trains mostly transported freight to businesses located along the line.

In many ways, the Santa Ana line is a microcosm of how the automobile eventually edged out the railroad as a preferred way to transport passengers and goods. In the 1990s, officials wanted to widen a nearby highway, meaning the railroad would lose its right of way.

The Santa Ana line was abandoned and now serves more as a hiker's destination than anything else.

But some of these hikers tell us that just because you abandon a rail line, the rail line doesn't necessarily abandon you. Folk tales and actual witness accounts still circulate—and maybe have even escalated—about the area's haunted activity and, in particular, a ghost train that still plows through this haunted section.

While walking along the path and taking pictures of the tracks, one witness wrote in *Backpackerverse*, a forum for hikers, that he heard what sounded like laughter. But you'll excuse him for not joining in: it wasn't that type of laughter. He described the sound as a bit creepy—sweet and naughty but not childish. The weird laughing sent a chill up his spine.

He initially thought he wanted to abandon his photographic hike.

"I wanted to turn away and leave," he wrote. "My friends were all heading back into town; I got my photographs of the tracks. After hours of shooting, I was ready to leave."

Then, something knocked him to the ground—he remained on his knees, unable to move. His camera fell, eventually resting a few feet away from him. He reached out for the camera, but it moved away from him. It was like something was pulling the camera away and down the railroad line.

Kneeling there in the middle of the tracks, the witness suddenly felt incredibly vulnerable. And the paranormal activity was just starting to heat up. He could feel it ramp up physically, emotionally, and spiritually.

"The laughter got louder; the air got hotter. Sweat broke along my spine, and my hands felt clammy. I shivered despite the heat."

The next moment, he heard something that he never expected to hear on a section of abandoned railroad tracks—the sound of metal wheels rolling along metal tracks. And it sounded like this ghost train was bearing down on him.

He hit the deck and prepared for the worst. The sound got louder and louder.

Fearing for his life and completely stunned by what he was experiencing, the witness managed to look up—and the shock only escalated.

"I did not want to look up, but I did not have a choice. There was a bright light, and I fell to my elbows, protecting my head. I couldn't lie down."

What kind of light? The light of an oncoming freight train?

He had no time to react and then felt heat all around him. He thought he was a goner, about to be hit by an oncoming phantom train.

"I was burning and suffocating," he added. "And then, it was gone. It was the longest minute of my life."

What's Behind the Haunting?

Stories about the abandoned tracks of the Santa Ana, like this one, sound exaggerated to the skeptic, and even the typically open-minded seeker, but the stories continue to intrigue paranormal enthusiasts. They wonder what could be behind a ghost train haunting.

They suggest a few theories. One of the leading theories suggests that hauntings are commonly linked to high-energy incidents. Violence and crime certainly fit the bill. And that section of California rail ran right through the wildest of the Wild West during its heyday. Gunfights and gamblers, robberies and horrific accidents are all part of the legacy of railroad history in Santa Ana. These paranormal buffs suggest that some of these incidents somehow became imprinted forever.

It's not just people who can become spirits, paranormal enthusiasts say. It could be that an entire locomotive becomes embedded in the time-space continuum.

Sounds crazy, right? That is, it sounds crazy until you're on your knees in the middle of Santa Ana's abandoned tracks listening to maniacal laughter and hearing the angry gnash of metal wheels grinding along metal tracks heading right toward you.

Do Famous Sci-Fi Writers Dream of Locomotive Spirits?

Point Reyes, California

There are a lot of witnesses to haunted railroad activity—train engineers and crew, rail workers, paranormal buffs, and just regular people who stumbled onto signs of the railroad's paranormal power. But our next witness is probably the most famous haunted railroad experiencer ever.

According to several accounts, Philip K. Dick, one of the world's most lauded science fiction authors and creator of *Through a Scanner Darkly* and *Do Androids Dream of Electric Sheep?*, said he believed ghost trains still traveled along a stretch of narrow gauge rails once operated by the North Pacific Coast Railroad.

The line once carried lumber, agricultural products, mail, and passengers from Sausalito to Cazadero. Before the construction of the Golden Gate Bridge, the passengers and freight would hop a ferry to cross the bay to San Francisco.

Towns along the route have a considerable haunted history. And they have every reason to be haunted. Shipwrecks, accidents, and conflict cut the history of the area just as deeply as the rocky crevices and cliffs gouge the rugged shoreline of the scenic coastline that the steam engines of the North Pacific Coast Railroad and other lines once carefully navigated.

One of the more famous pieces of railroad ghostlore centers on a stretch of Marin Shore Railroad and the vengeful spirit of an angry railroad engineer who lost his most precious cargo: his daughter.

According to the story, which appeared in a Northwestern Pacific Railroad magazine in 1928, the engineer, named Mahoney, once lived in a camp in White Hill, California, a community settled by many railroad workers. Mahoney was a single father. His wife had died unexpectedly, leaving him alone to raise their beautiful daughter. Single-parenting is difficult enough today—imagine what it was like in the late nineteenth century. But he tried his best. Unfortunately, he couldn't be everywhere at once and his job frequently took him far away for long stretches of time. The sweet, beautiful young lady drew the attention of many suitors. She met a man, who became her boyfriend. Eventually, the engineer's daughter became pregnant. And then her boyfriend abandoned her.

Mahoney's treasured daughter died during childbirth.

The townsfolk said Mahoney's fury could not be soothed. He spent the rest of his life seeking to exact revenge on his daughter's lover.

They say he is still looking.

People say that they have seen a ghost train—sometimes called the Fairfax Ghost Train—appear on stormy nights, just like the night that his dear daughter departed this world. They say it's old Mahoney still seeking to avenge her death.

It's a great piece of railroad folklore, but Philip K. Dick—or PKD, for short—who once lived in the area where the ghost story of Mahoney was told, may have had his own encounter with Mahoney, or, at least had a brush with another ghostly reminder of the region's railroad past. Dick had an on-again, off-again relationship with the paranormal, according to biographers. At times, the writer claimed to have experienced time slips and predicted the future. He even believed he used these powers to miraculously diagnosis his child's illness. At other times, he completely discounted psychic powers.

In a biography of the sci-fi writer, however, his former wife, Anne Dick, wrote that PKD had a few ghost stories. For example, he once saw the ghost of an elderly Italian man in his residence. The couple lived in the Point Reyes Station, where PKD did some of his most prolific writing, and the writer complained of hearing trains—ghost trains, to be exact. On windy nights, PKD told his wife he could hear the sound of steam engines chugging through Point Reyes Station. Indeed, narrow gauge trains did use tracks to move people and freight in and out of the town. There's one problem with his report, though: narrow gauge trains ceased operations in the early 1900s, decades before the couple moved into the area.

Anne had a better explanation: it was the powerful winds that swept off the coast that made the steam train-like sounds.

It seems like a natural explanation, but with the stories of ghosts and tales of vengeful railroad spirits that sweep over this area just as powerfully as the coastal breeze, is that theory a little too simple to discount the idea that one of the world's most perceptive, paranormally prone fantasy writers possibly tapped into the sounds of Point Reyes Station's railroad past?

Ghost Train or Eerie Railroad Premonition?

Alberta, Canada

In the early twentieth century, it took a special person to serve as a crew member on board a speeding wagon of steel, iron, steam, and fire that we call a locomotive. A fireman, one of those train crew members, didn't put out fires on board the train; he kept them lit so the powerful engine could keep the wheels churning toward the train's ultimate destination. A railroad fireman, whose main duty was to shovel coal into a steam engine's firebox, had to be smart, tough, strong, and willing to put up with long hours away from friends and family.

One fireman, however, discovered it took more than brains and brawn to be a member of a locomotive crew. It also apparently required nerves steady enough to withstand a direct encounter with the ultimate strangeness of railroad paranormal activity.

According to our next story—which comes from *Spooky Canada*, S. E. Schlosser's book on railroad folklore legends, and a newspaper account of the incident—a series of horrific encounters haunted a fireman for the rest of his life.

The story begins on a May night of 1908. According to Andrew Staysko, a fireman on the Canadian Pacific Railway, he and the rest of the crew were about three kilometers (just under two miles) away from Medicine Hat when they noticed something strange on the horizon. A light appeared directly in front of them. And there was no mistaking it, the light looked like a headlamp of a rapidly approaching locomotive. The light grew larger and brighter with each passing second. There was no doubt now; the two trains were on a collision course without any hope for evasive action. The engineer reasoned that trying to stop the train would be pointless. It didn't look like the oncoming train was trying to slow down, either. The engineer was a well-respected man named Twohey, one of the best engineers in the company. He yelled at his fireman to jump, with the hope that he would leap clear of what would soon be an inevitable mangled mess of metal.

But Staysko didn't have time. He stood helplessly watching as the light from the approaching train barreled straight for him and his train.

For those last few seconds, the fireman contemplated his own mortality.

And then, when all seemed to be lost, the oncoming engine miraculously swerved to the right and continued on its path on rails parallel to the fireman's train. That only troubled the poor fireman more because there were no parallel train tracks. This was a single-track line, Staysko stated. The crew watched as the ghost train eerily passed by them. They even saw the passengers in the ghost train staring back at them.

The ghost train let out an ear-shattering, heaven-piercing shriek of its horn. And just like that, it was gone.

According to Staysko, the crew made it to their destination unharmed and in one piece, but the incident had caused a great deal of damage, mainly psychological damage. Twohey decided to take some time off to recover. When he finally came back to his job as engineer, he asked to be assigned to work in the railyard, at least temporarily. At that time, the shock was still fresh in his mind and he had no desire to take command of a train that might cross paths with the ghost train that haunted the hills outside of town.

While the incident seriously scared Staysko, he decided not to give up his position. A fireman, after all, was a step on the fast track toward a career as a higher-paid engineer.

A few weeks later his ambition would again be tested. This time he tended the fire onboard a train headed by an engineer named J. Nicholson. While the engineer was different, the route was uncomfortably familiar. Again, the train chugged along on the tracks outside of Medicine Hat in the depth of night. They were right about where the first incident with the ghost train had occurred when the screech of a train whistle broke the silence of the cool night air.

The fireman looked out the window and thought it must be déjà vu. The bright light of an approaching train flooded the cab of the engine. And, just as before, an eerie visage of a train appeared right in front of the crew and a head-on collision seemed imminent.

The locomotive phantom, though, snapped to the right and ran alongside the train, as it did a few weeks prior. Nicholson and the fireman saw the same grim expressions etched on the faces of the passengers as the train faded into the night.

That was enough.

Promotion or no promotion, the fireman asked to be transferred temporarily to the yard division. That's where he worked throughout the late spring and early summer before summoning up the courage to assume the role of fireman again.

One evening in early July, he was in the yard firing up an engine when he heard the devastating news. Two trains had collided outside of Medicine Hat. Staysko recognized from the description that the accident must have happened near the spot where he had his supernatural encounter with the ghost train.

Then he heard the names of the engineers: the engineer of the oncoming train was Bob Twohey.

At the helm of the second train?

Engineer J. Nicholson.

Scary Scandinavian Ghost Train

Stockholm, Sweden

Swedes sensed something different about the train, almost menacing. It stood out. Most trains in the Stockholm Metro service back in the 1960s were painted green. This train, though, shimmered in a silver sheen that inspired the train's nickname, Silverpilen—or the Silver Bullet.

Built as a test model, manufacturers only produced one Silver Bullet. Swedes are probably happy about that. Ever since the construction of the flashy silver train, urban legends began to circulate that the train possessed supernatural powers, and even long after the model was discontinued and taken off the line, sightings of the eight-car Silver Bullet continue. And, what's even freakier, this silver-colored ghost train has even been implicated in a series of mysterious time slips.

But first, let's talk about the ghostly appearance of the Silverpilen. According to numerous sources and witnesses, people claim to be minding their own business at a train station when they see and hear a train approaching, usually coming in from out of the mist. This train, however, doesn't look like the other trains on the line—and it sounds much different. The Silverpilen, it should be pointed out, had a special motor that produced a "whining" sound. That's exactly how the ghost train witnesses describe the sound of this phantom on rails.

Often, stories from these witnesses suggest that despite the strange look and weird noises, they don't give the train too much thought. Just another train. However, that indifference turns into complete astonishment when they watch the train pass by them and disappear into the mist.

Skeptics, of course, have a meteorological explanation—the train just becomes covered by a thick fog. It doesn't actually disappear.

Or does it? A few witnesses claim that the train doesn't just physically disappear; the sound of its engine abruptly stops as well.

And there are other accounts that indicate it's more than just a blanket of mist that covers the train. The Silverpilen, somehow, is able to mask time and space. There are a few rumors of people who mistaken the silver bullet train for their ride and hop on. Oddly, when they exit the train, they say that they lost time—a five-minute ride took twenty minutes, for example. Fog might be dense, but can it warp the very nature of time?

More ominously, a few reports—unconfirmed, as far as I can tell—say there are people who got on the Silverpilen and never got off. Never.

While the Silverpilen has long been taken off the rails, the stories—or the urban legends, depending on where you fall on the supernatural belief spectrum—continue. In fact, this funky new train is considered one of Sweden's biggest unsolved supernatural mysteries.

— Chapter 2 —
HAUNTED CABOOSES

You don't see those old cabooses traveling the rails like you used to, but at one time, the venerable cars brought up the rear of a train as surely as a period rides at the end of a sentence.

Times have changed and, due to new technologies, the caboose has become irrelevant. Crews no longer need a command center, which is basically what the caboose served as. Over time, train companies sold their cabooses, or just scrapped them. For some entrepreneurs, though, the cool-looking, almost romantic-looking, living spaces on rails made a tempting business prospect. They believed that they could turn the caboose into hotel rooms. What a lot of these entrepreneurs didn't know was that the caboose is the railroad equivalent of a haunted house. Crews basically lived in cabooses, and those living quarters apparently became after-life living quarters for the ghosts of railroad crew members, and even some passengers.

In the next few pages, you'll visit just some of the cabooses, which may have been the last car in the train but is definitely not last in tales of haunted trains and train cars.

Possessed Caboose

Topeka, Kansas

By this point in the book, you probably already have some sense that nearly all haunted railroad stories can be a bit hard to believe at times. But even among the tales of the strange and unbelievable, you'll find some haunted rail tales are really unbelievable, like our next one: a story about a spirit-driven caboose. Yet, strangely, there have been credible witnesses who seem to back up these outlandish claims.

Just like other pieces of haunted railroad equipment, cabooses are said to be home to spirits. In previous tales, we have reviewed stories about ghost trains—the ghostly engines pulling cars that can appear one moment and just as easily vanish the next. Our next story about a ghost caboose is different. Way different. The witnesses to this bizarre phenomenon—first reported in the late nineteenth century—claimed that a caboose wasn't just haunted by a spirit; it was, in some ways, a spirit itself. And the caboose didn't pop in and out of existence, like some of the haunted trains we've discussed. No, this caboose was real enough. However, witnesses said the caboose could do weird things, like drive itself down rails and even defy the laws of physics by chugging up and over hills (remember, cabooses aren't self-propelled). The story is told in the pages of *Topeka State Journal.*

According to the newspaper article, railroad workers for the Louisville and Nashville (L&N) railroad began to notice something was amiss with a caboose that had recently been involved in a horrible accident. Each tale about the caboose—number 1908—became increasingly more bizarre. Witnesses said that old 1908 would shimmy and shake while the train was stopped and otherwise motionless. It would jump and lurch, even when it stood alone on the track.

Perhaps the most incredible tale about the 1908 occurred when it decided it no longer needed a locomotive to drag it around anymore. It could violate the laws of physics on its own, thank you very much. One day, while the caboose sat on a side track in Richmond, Virginia, workers said the caboose suddenly lurched into operation, traveled down the track, up a hill, over an embankment, and into a nearby field. What's even weirder: when the men ran to the scene, they confirmed that all of the brakes were set.

But the men had known old 1908's haunted behavior a long time before that incident. Crews who rode in the caboose reminded people that this was the same caboose that would start to shake and hop at odd moments.

The idea that 1908 seemed to have a mind and a life of its own was no longer a question for the workers of the L&N. They wanted to know why the caboose was possessed, or, more precisely, who possessed the caboose.

A few theories swirled around about the possessed caboose. One explanation, though, climbed to the top of how a normal old railroad caboose suddenly became possessed. According to the newspaper, years before the activity began, a train pulling freight cars and old 1908 ran over a man right outside of Lexington. It's believed that the spirit of this man possesses the caboose. As proof, theorists cite an incident that occurred at the crossing of the Russell Cave pike, the spot where the fatal accident occurred years earlier. Witnesses said that as the train carrying 1908 pulled through the crossing, it suddenly stopped. A few seconds of silence and stillness passed. Then, old 1908 began to "quiver and shake and crawl and creep like a man who had just awakened from a hideous nightmare," the newspaper stated. Meanwhile, the rest of the train never budged and seemed unaffected by whatever "vibrations" had possessed its caboose.

The strange activity continued, according to the newspaper account.

"The lanterns and lamps danced up and down and flickered and waved viciously though not a breath of air was stirring," the newspaper reports. "The brake beams and rods under old '1908' groaned and creaked, though no other sound came from any other part of the train."

This whole incident was terrifying enough for the train's crew, but things would turn even creepier.

Just as old 1908 settled down and the train began to resume its journey, the men claimed they heard a horrifying scream. The shriek didn't come from in the caboose. It came from under it.

They only had a few seconds to process this horrifying event when more unexplainable activity broke out. They said that the caboose began to jump up and down on the tracks "as if to escape some tormentor."

Who the tormentor was, the men could only offer guesses. But the crew, who had years of railroad experience, knew a few things for sure. They knew of no other force that could shake a solidly built caboose, or lift it off the tracks. Whatever force caused the phenomena didn't seem to be related to any natural occurrence that they had experienced in their careers. Skeptics might suggest a minor earthquake, or the work of a few trickster coworkers, but none of those explanations satisfied the men.

While the ghost of old 1908 seemed to fade into history, these men, no doubt, went on telling stories to generations of new railroad workers about their encounter with not a haunted caboose, necessarily, but a ghost-possessed caboose.

Haunted Caboose, Female Ghost

Rockford, Kentucky

Let's face it: some haunted railroad cars are just luckier than others. In haunted railroad lore you have ghosts of rough-and-tough yard workers, a bunch of spirits of hard-working brakemen—some with a few limbs missing—and even the specters of some decapitated conductors. But a caboose, number 17,736—owned by a Kentucky railroad—had a far more elegant, and a far more reliable apparition gracing the crew quarters.

Reports that a female ghost haunted the caboose came from an impeccable source. J. H. Riley, a seasoned and well-regarded conductor for a couple of railroad companies, said the ghost of a woman frequently appeared at the same window seat in the rear of the caboose. Riley got a good look at the woman. He described her as slender and pale with a "sad, though beautiful, face." The spirit had some fashion sense, too, sporting a broad-brimmed hat that perfectly suited her elegant countenance.

An account, which appeared in the July 6, 1888, issue of the *Enquirer*, adds, "The dress and garments are plain and modest and impress one with the belief that the owner was formerly a neatly attired lady and had, perhaps, been making a brief call on friends."

Riley had such a good look at the woman because, unlike most ghosts who appear and disappear on a whim, this spirit would stay in the caboose for hours as long as she wasn't disturbed. Usually, the ghost appeared when no one was in the caboose, but she could be seen through the caboose's external and internal windows. As soon as someone opened the door to the caboose or rushed up the steps, she typically vanished.

This is a caboose used by the Michigan Central Railroad between 1900 and 1920.

The testimony of the conductor is bolstered by his status as a former skeptic. The apparition first tested, then blasted through, his skepticism, he told the reporters. When Riley first saw the ghost, he immediately investigated, trying to debunk the phenomena. He had the entire interior of the caboose carefully examined, looking for any natural explanations. Riley and his coworkers never found any way that the ghostly image of the woman could be an optical illusion—such as a weird reflection off the window, for example, or an errant shadow falling on the seat.

But they knew what they had seen.

Throughout the years, crews would get especially jumpy when the train was forced to stop during its trips through the mystical and spooky mountains of Kentucky. Crews said that when the train paused, they heard strange noises in the caboose, noises that didn't seem to have any natural source.

Other witnesses stepped forward. According to the newspaper account, many citizens of the Kentucky town who, like Riley, also had impeccable reputations, said they also saw the ghost of the lady. One man said he didn't just see the ghost but spoke with her. He said she spoke with him in a very sorrowful tone before she started to cry. Another man said the spirit followed him out of the caboose and gestured for him to return. When he did, she had disappeared, but laughter echoed throughout the caboose.

Long before people began to charge to visit haunted houses, the caboose kind of became a paranormal tourist attraction. People gathered along the tracks to watch caboose number 17,736 chug by. Some said they saw what looked like a misty apparition float out of the window of the caboose and fly "through the space like the fairies of an enchanted tale."

The haunting of 17,736 caused such a stir that, logically, people began to speculate just whose spirit was haunting the caboose. According to the *Enquirer*'s story, people believed a woman who was injured in a railroad-related accident lived long enough to issue a curse on her deathbed. She said that as revenge for taking her life, she would haunt the railroad and its men. Other theories are less ominous. For instance, there is a theory that the woman is the wife of a man who died in an accident and who later died herself, the victim of a broken heart.

Several witnesses have stepped forward to corroborate the latter explanation for the haunting, according to the article. The witnesses—family members of the deceased lovesick woman—claim that they had been near the caboose when they heard the voice of a female sorrowfully calling out the name of her departed husband. They immediately knew it was the voice of their dead relative.

There are other strange stories attached to the ghost of 17,736. For instance, a legend grew that if a person disturbed the ghost of the caboose as she sat in her favorite seat, bad things would follow. The ghost, it seems, had a power to curse.

Besides this one newspaper article, it's hard to find much more information about the haunted caboose. Old 17,736—and the broken-hearted woman—seem to have finally and, hopefully, restfully faded away.

Haunted Caboose Hotels

The dependable old caboose tagged along at the end of a train like a faithful pet. But it had several important functions. For example, conductors used the caboose as a mobile office to fill out paperwork. Crews staffed the caboose to stand watch from the cupola, checked on brakes, and generally got some rest. As mentioned, technology replaced most of these duties, and cabooses, one of the endearing pieces of the railroading operation, finally faded into obsolescence.

Sadly, many cabooses headed not to a well-deserved retirement for their faithful service, but to the scrap yard. Some remain, rusting away in railyards.

But other entrepreneurs felt the nostalgia people had for the caboose and sensed an opportunity. As mentioned previously, these entrepreneurs saw that these former railroad crew quarters would make excellent rooms for travelers as an attractive alternative to the same-old hotel and bed-and-breakfast stays. These railroad rescuers bought the cabooses—fairly inexpensively—and reconditioned them to their former glory.

A lot of these entrepreneurs had no idea that the sale of the relics included a different sort of railroad relic—spirits of the country's locomotive past.

Featherbed Inn

Upper Lake, California

Located in the heart of California's wine country, Featherbed Inn features nine vintage railroad cabooses that serve as rooms for guests. The owners decorated each caboose to reflect a theme, such as "Orient Express," "Casablanca," and the "Wild, Wild West." Each caboose has an individual style and flare. And some of these pieces of railroad past and hotel future have ghosts.

Although it's hard to say when the hauntings started, the current owners, June and Paul Vejar, said the ghosts were intact when they purchased the property. Guests and staff have recorded their run-ins with the paranormal at the Featherbed Inn for the past few years.

The ghosts are suspected in a series of mystifying events at the inn. The windows on the Santa Fe and Southern Pacific cabooses appear to be the focus of paranormal activities. Guests have closed the windows and then, a few moments later, find that someone has opened them again, even though no one else was with them in the caboose. Even the owners report this activity.

"When we first bought the place I would walk by one of the cabooses and the window would be open," June said in a promotional video about the hotel. "There was nobody in there. I would go back in and shut the window. I'd walk back by and the window was open again. This went on for a couple of months and they finally, I guess, decided to not mess with me anymore."

The owners also notice that objects, like soap and toiletries, appear to teleport. They set the soap down in one bathroom, then they go back to check on the room and the soap has disappeared, only to reappear in the bathroom of another caboose.

Closet doors have also been known to open and close by themselves.

While skeptics might attribute this activity to typical maintenance issues with old railroad relics, or just absent-minded guests and hoteliers, other phenomena are harder to explain away. The phantom footsteps are a good example. One guest told the owners that a disturbing noise woke her from a restful sleep. She heard the pounding of feet coming up the steps to the caboose she had rented. The footsteps sounded purposeful. At first, the guest thought her husband had returned from his morning walk, but when she looked out the window, there was no one there—and her husband returned much later, so it wasn't him.

The guest realized something else: if the ghost had walked up the steps to her door, he might still have been in the room with her because she had never heard him leave.

"And she didn't hear anyone walk back down," June said. "She just heard footsteps coming up."

One apparition has been reported too. Witnesses have claimed to see a man in a striped suit, but his identity remains somewhat of a mystery. And, while the ghost or ghosts haunting the cabooses are not always seen, people say they can be heard. Some guests say they can plainly hear someone call their name, but when they look around the caboose, there's no one there.

So, who's haunting the inn? There are a few guesses. Former owners of the property are among the suspects behind the paranormal activity. Other people suggest the cabooses are haunted by railroad workers who once lived and toiled in the cabooses.

The Canyon Motel

Williams, Arizona

Owners of another popular destination that converted cabooses into motel rooms have a similar problem—or opportunity, depending on the guest's willingness to confront the weird and unexplained. The owners of the Canyon Motel in Williams, Arizona, say their guests and members of the staff have reported strange activity after their stay in Caboose #2.

Guests and motel workers have compiled a long list of paranormal phenomena in the caboose, including strange noises, lights and lamps that turn on and off by themselves, and moving objects. A housekeeper said she could hear people talking and whispering in the caboose during the middle of the day when the room was completely empty.

There's even a report that an apparition of a man, who looks as though he's dressed as a railroad conductor from years ago, wanders through the caboose swinging a lantern.

— Chapter 3 —

HAUNTED RAILROAD MUSEUMS

The first stop on our ride along the haunted rails begins in Altoona, Pennsylvania. Not just because Altoona is about an hour from my current home and served as the "big city" when I was growing up, but because it's a place that is nearly synonymous with railroad history.

But that's not the only reason.

Whereas some towns have a haunted railroad station or a cursed railroad crossing, the whole city of Altoona seems haunted. The city's reputation for ghosts and spirits make it one of the most haunted spots in Pennsylvania and, possibly, the country. Because the railroad played an integral role in the city—so much so that Altoona was once referred to as the railroad capital of the world—it's no surprise that many of those ghost stories are attached to the region's many railroad landmarks.

Our exploration of the haunted railroad places begins with a look at a monument to Altoona's railroad history, the Railroaders Memorial Museum, which has collected lots of historic artifacts from the region and country's railroad past and, apparently, a bunch of haunted artifacts.

The Railroaders Memorial Museum

Altoona, Pennsylvania

According to a now-legendary Altoona ghost story, at the end of a hard day, the former finance director of the Railroaders Memorial Museum walked from his fourth-floor office of the museum to the building's elevator. The fourth floor is a quiet section of the stoic brick building that was once part of the Penn Central Railroad shop complex, situated in the heart of Altoona's once-bustling railroad hub. The fourth floor is typically off-limits to visitors and a special key is needed to access it.

The Railroaders Memorial Museum is shown in the foreground of this panoramic view of Altoona, Pennsylvania; date unknown.

This evening was anything but typical for the director. And someone didn't need a special key to access the floor.

The finance director said that as the elevator door swung open, he hopped in, just like he had hundreds of times before. Because he's usually the last one in the office, he's often the only one in the elevator—and, more than likely, the only one in the whole building. On this ride, however, the executive found that he wasn't alone. A man stood on the other side of the elevator with his back to him. Slowly, this unexpected guest casually looked over his shoulder at the dismayed finance director. He had no idea who this stranger was.

As the executive stood there, speechless, the man's body started to shimmy electrically.

And just as suddenly, the man vanished.

Investigation at the Museum

The story of the financial director's ghostly run-in joins dozens, maybe hundreds, of paranormal encounters reported by staff and visitors, along with pages of ghostlore written about the museum. Paranormal investigators John Albert and Beth Ann Karle, of JABA Paranormal (the initials derive from the investigators' first initials), are in the enviable—or unenviable, depending on your openness to the supernatural—position of serving as key investigators into the weird happenings at the museum, Altoona's living tribute to the city's railroaders of past and present.

In a personal interview, John said that he and his wife have been investigating the paranormal since 2009. TV shows like *Ghost Hunters* spurred on much of John's interest in the paranormal, while Beth is a natural empath, meaning she has a deep connection to the spirit world. The combination of Beth's spiritual side and John's more analytical side gives the couple a unique tool box of both scientific and spiritual instruments they can use to investigate hauntings, John suggested. The team has produced some of the most compelling accounts of supernatural phenomena at the museum, according to many familiar with the haunting.

According to John, the team has had run-ins with shadow figures and the ghost of a young girl. They may have even had chats with other spirits that roam through the museum, but it's the ghost of the girl who seems to be the most willing to talk to and interact with the investigators.

On one investigation, JABA members zeroed in on the gift shop as a possible center for paranormal activity. Using dowsing rods, members tried to make contact with a spirit in the shop. The way John explains it, a person holds the rod and another investigator asks the spirit questions. How the rod moves indicates the spirit's answer to the question. In the gift shop, one spirit got a little wild with the answers. During a spirited question-and-answer session, a ghost seemed to communicate with the team. The session revealed that the ghost of a girl who haunts the gift shop was young, but they're not sure of her age or why she inhabits that spot in particular. They get the sense from their interaction that she's a playful spirit.

"She loves playing with me during the investigations," said John. "She will spin one of the rods in circles very fast."

The information gathered at the gift shop seems to corroborate other weird events people have reported at this section of the museum. For instance, one morning, gift shop workers opened up and stepped into their shop only to find that every single item was taken from the shelves and placed on the floor. Nothing was stolen, however.

Who would spend all that time sneaking into a place and then waste all of that time gently placing items on the floor? The ghost of a playful little girl, believers answer.

In another investigation a male spirit came through, according to John. This ghost may act as a guardian, of sorts, of the spirit of the young girl. The encounter happened during an investigation on the museum's third floor. As the team swept through the area, using the dowsing rods to attempt to contact any spirits in that spot, they began to receive indications that a spirit was present. As JABA members began to ask questions, they say the spirit of a man began to make contact. He even showed the team his picture!

"This last time we were there, we were on the third floor and were talking to one man and found out his picture was one on the wall of the room we were in," John said. "He used the rods to point to his picture, and we had two people holding rods and both sets of rods pointed to the same picture."

John explained that the team tries to use several sets of dowsing rods to verify contact. They believe that if rods held by two people behave similarly, it increases the likelihood that they established real contact and that it's not mere coincidence. They also invite non-team members who go along on investigations to use the rods to independently verify their results.

"We allow the public to use the rods so they see we are not manipulating them ourselves and we have even sat back-to-back so neither person can see how the other's rods are responding," said John.

As they continued to use the dowsing rods to interview the ghost, other details began to emerge about the connection between the ghost of the older man and the young girl's spirit the team had met in the gift shop.

"We found out that the girl in the gift shop is watched over by a man," said John. "The man is not mean to the girl, but does not like when she interacts with me. That came as heartbreaking news to me, as she always seems very active with me."

They are pretty sure, however, that the spirit is not the same as yet another ghost that haunts the museum, perhaps the most famous of the facility's many ghosts. Most people just call him Frank.

Famous—or Infamous—Frank

Frank is a bit of a standout for the many spirits who haunt the museum. While most of the spirits tend to be shy and only communicate with the living through dowsing rods and subtle signs and noises, Frank has appeared to startled visitors and staff—like the finance director in the elevator. According to experts on the haunting, Frank especially loves to show up during public tours and when ghost hunters investigate the premises. He also likes to freak out the volunteers and workers.

In one story, a woman who was working at the museum's gift shop—located near the entry of the building—noticed a stranger lingering around one of the main exhibits in the building. Whoever it was, this person was engaged in activities that were decidedly off-limits for most workers and volunteers—and were certainly not permitted for visitors. The woman watched the man crawl all over one of the train engines on display near the museum's entrance. It was baffling enough that the guy had the effrontery to violate the rules of decorum for a museum guest, but the way he was climbing on the engine gave this woman pause. He really knew what he was doing, like he had been working on this engine all his life.

She had no idea.

As she watched, the man dropped over the side of the engine—and simply vanished.

The woman later said she believed that she had an encounter with Frank. After all, her description matched up with other Frank encounters, like the ghostly figure who shared the elevator ride with a museum executive.

In another encounter, possibly with the phantom Frank, a paranormal skeptic visited the museum. He was, in fact, a regular visitor there. He said that after touring the third floor, he took a seat near the lab area. Another man started walking toward him. Nothing peculiar about that, but the skeptic did notice the man wore clothes from a bygone era and an out-of-style hat. The skeptic turned for a second and looked back.

The strangely dressed man had disappeared.

Hoping to hold on to his skepticism, the man asked a worker who else was in the building with him.

The answer wasn't what he wanted to hear. He was alone. Well, maybe not alone-alone. Frank was with him.

Why Frank?

So, how did Frank get his name?

Most experts on the museum's hauntings say that's simple: Frank showed them his picture. After the financial director's story spread among the staff, some of the museum's employees led the director to a group of pictures of workers and he immediately pointed to a group photo showing a gang of steam boiler workers from the 1920s. He singled out one particular individual in the shot and said that this was the guy he shared his elevator with, according to numerous sources on the haunting.

But, here's the thing: the executive pointed out the same man in the same picture that other people picked out after their own chance meeting with the long-dead railroader.

And the man's name, according to the picture's caption, was Frank.

More Haunted Happenings

Frank and the little girl are only the lead car in a long train of paranormal phenomena reported in the museum. JABA, for example, has collected other evidence in various spots of the museum. One of the spookiest bits of evidence indicates that a shadow figure—also called a shadow person—lurks in the halls. Well-known in paranormal lore, these inky black spirits are often linked to more negative types of hauntings, although there doesn't seem to be evidence of any malevolent action from the museum's shadow figure, the team suggests.

John said that the team investigated reports that on numerous occasions people have seen shadow figures moving on the far side of the bridged area on the second floor of the building. The paranormal investigators placed a specific type of technology, called a shadow detector, in the spot where people reported seeing the figure. The detector can sense when the light changes in an area. A sudden change in the light pattern, the team hypothesizes, means a shadow figure could be near. During one investigation, the detector signaled an alert. The investigators made everyone near the detector stop to see if their shadows could have caused the reaction in the equipment. John said they tried to debunk it, but failed to find any natural cause.

"Nothing we did would cause the detector to activate, bringing us to the conclusion that there was something moving around in that area that was not a living person," John reported.

He added that JABA members heard evidence of the haunting, too.

"We've experienced the sound of a glass sliding across the counter in the bar," he said. "We have had what sounded like a cabinet open behind the bar, with no one behind there and nothing actually moved. We've heard laughter in the corner of the gift shop where there were no people."

Other witnesses said they heard big band music being piped into the museum, particularly in "Kelly's Bar," an exhibit designed to give the visitor an idea of what a railroader bar was really like back in the industry's heyday. But, there's one problem with that; the museum doesn't pipe any music into that exhibit. In fact, they don't play music in any section.

The phantom music, witnesses say, is a haunting melody, in more ways than one.

So Why Is the Museum Haunted?

As you'll see in numerous examples throughout this book, railroad history is synonymous with haunted history. Wherever they build a railroad, ghosts and ghostlore soon follow. But why does this museum in Altoona, in particular, seem to harbor so many ghosts? Many paranormal theorists suggest that the building is, first, pretty old. Built more than a century ago, the building probably acquired a lot of spiritual baggage over that century-plus of existence to serve the needs of the railroad industry. Others say the building's temporary duties—it was used at various times as an infirmary and as the Pennsylvania Railroad's police station—probably generated enough strife and tragedy to explain a lot of the current supernatural activity.

Others say that Altoona is just a haunted hotspot. In the pages ahead, you'll read about more hauntings in the Altoona area; some are related to the city's railroad history, but some are not.

There's still some debate about whether the Railroaders Memorial Museum is haunted at all. Skeptics say that the haunting is pretty easy to explain. Old buildings with lots of history look haunted. When people visit them, they are more likely to misinterpret natural phenomena as supernatural phenomena. That door closing by itself? It's just the wind. Shadows dancing across the walls? They're just shadows, or tricks of the mind.

The team from television's *Ghost Hunters* conducted an investigation of the museum and came up, basically, empty. They did not find any evidence of paranormal powers at work in the building. Despite that, JABA and other ghost hunting aficionados, along with visitors and staff, continue to gather evidence and discuss incidents that suggest maybe the television team just happened to pick a quiet day for the spirits at the museum.

After all, even railroad ghosts deserve a day off every now and then.

Has a Haunted Hobo Boarded a Railroad Museum Without a Pass?

Belleville, Ohio

Guests and workers at the Mad River and NKP Railroad Museum say more than a few ghosts have taken an afterlife ride in the building, but at least one of them probably did not pay for a ticket. NKP, by the way, is the reporting mark for Nickel Plate Road, a railroad that served the mid-central U.S.

According to a group of paranormal investigators, one of the ghosts that haunt the Bellevue, Ohio, museum might be the ghost of one of the world's most famous hobos: Steam Train Maury. Maury Graham, who died in 2006, made it his mission to preserve the memory of the band of people that writer John Steinbeck called "the last free men on earth"—the itinerant railroad riders we usually politically incorrectly refer to as hobos.

While Graham, the five-time King of the Hobos, tried to preserve the memory of the hobo by writing about his times riding the rail and the people he met, he also served as an unofficial hobo spokesperson, offering countless interviews to the press.

There's another way Steam Train Maury helps to keep the hobo legend living on—he simply refuses to take that last train to the afterlife. Many think that Graham is behind at least some of the haunted activity that takes place in the museum, which has hundreds of railroad artifacts on display, featuring everything from engines, cabooses, and World War II–era sleeper cars to uniforms, linens, and railroad timetables. Believers in the Steam Train Maury ghost believe his spirit is attached to one of the cabooses stored at the museum. They say that his ghost has appeared on the back of one of the cabooses in particular.

While Steam Train Maury haunts the caboose, the whole museum has its share of spooky activity. According to Ruth Fuehring, Mad River and NKP Railroad Society trustee, visitors and workers have heard strange sounds and voices echoing in the halls of the museum.

"We've had people tell us they hear voices from the cars," Fuehring told Shop Bellevue Ohio, a Bellevue events website. "A lot of people say it gives them the spooks when they come here and hear those voices."

People reported so much paranormal activity so often that the museum officials called in some experts. A few of the paranormal teams confirmed these spirit interactions. The researchers, too, heard strange noises—and even a few more terrifying sounds.

"At one point a few years ago the investigators could hear someone screaming for help in the museum," Fuehring reported. "There are a lot of strange, interesting things that can happen when investigating the paranormal."

Not all the haunted activity in the museum can be seen or heard. Some must be felt, Fuehring indicated. Guests and workers report weird feelings at certain times and at certain places in the museum. For instance, people say they experienced a sensation like they're being watched while in the museum. Others just spontaneously feel creeped out for no apparent reason.

While the society trustee has never had a run-in with an actual ghost, she can affirm much of the phenomena at the museum.

"I've never actually seen anything, but sometimes I'll hear a voice or feel like I'm being watched when I'm there at night," Fuehring said. "I believe in that stuff, but some people are more sensitive to it than I am."

A group called Ohio Researchers of Banded Spirits, or ORBS, investigated the site. The team, which has appeared on television shows such as *My Ghost Story* and *The Haunted*, said they collected some EVP while checking out the museum. One of the team members suggested in an article on Mental Floss that because spirits can sometimes attach themselves to objects like uniforms, or even the King of the Hobos' favorite caboose, railroad museums that collect a lot of these objects, like the Mad River and NKP Railroad museum, may be a sort of passenger station house for several spirits.

"Spirits can attach themselves to certain items," Karlo Zuzic, a paranormal investigator and project manager for ORBS, told Mental Floss.

Waves of Paranormal Phenomena

Laupahoehoe, Hawaii

On the morning of April 1, 1946, news began to sweep across Hawaii that a series of massive waves had hit the Laupahoehoe peninsula on the northeast section of Hawaii's big island, essentially wiping an entire town off the map.

Most residents thought this was a horribly inappropriate April Fool's joke.

Later, they soon discovered the awful truth: the news was no joke at all—a tsunami had actually smashed the shore of the quiet section of the island and killed about 160 people. Like a ravenous monster, the wave grabbed some of the bodies off of dry land and pulled them back into the sea. The railroad, which was so painstakingly constructed along the shore to help transport sugar cane from the fields to Hilo, bore the brunt of the waves, according to sources. The tsunami smashed bridges, trestles, and buildings. The tsunami also wiped an engine right off the tracks.

Essentially, the tsunami destroyed the railroad industry in the area. It couldn't recover. But the railroad workers haven't disappeared—not completely, at least. Staff members of the Laupahoehoe Train Museum and their visitors continue to collect evidence that the ghosts of the tsunami victims still haunt Laupahoehoe—

and that the departed railroad workers, specifically, haunt the building and grounds of the museum.

Witnesses claim to hear weird noises when they're in the building. Late at night, or when the museum is quiet, people hear the sounds of footsteps pacing up and down the halls. When they walk toward the spot where they think the sounds originated, they're stumped to find the area is empty. There's no one else in the hall.

Some people even claim to hear music playing, but there are no radios or stereos turned on. The music seems like it's coming from nowhere, or maybe from heaven.

While many railroad museums admit that their buildings are haunted—which this section of the book proves—the train museum at Laupahoehoe has made considerable efforts to document the paranormal activity. Over the years, the museum has gathered a sizeable collection of pictures taken by visitors and volunteers that seem to show shapes and images; the visitors and volunteers believe this to be evidence that ghosts haunt the premises. Based on these photographs, the ghosts have primarily attached themselves to several areas in the building and in a few displays located on the grounds of the museum.

Paranormal experts who have investigated the museum suggest that the most haunted spot in the building is the train conductor's office. At first glance, one photo taken in the office appears to show a man in a railroad conductor's costume. The weirdest thing is that the man's costume seems to be of a much earlier period. It's too authentic, believers say, speculating that this is no man in a costume. In other words, this is a ghost in an actual conductor's uniform.

Another photo shows a foggy form hovering near the piano that's on display. The form stretches about midway up the piano into the ceiling of the room. Speculation is that this apparition might be the pianist who likes to entertain guests with spooky music.

When the photographer who visited the museum snapped a picture of the couch in the museum, they probably just wanted a shot of the original furnishings to show friends and family. But a group of ghosts seems to have photobombed that picture. Some people say it's a group of railroad workers on break.

Before the building became a museum, it served as the home of a train conductor. A few people think the ghost of the conductor's son still haunts the place. A picture does seem to show a transparent image of a young boy staring wistfully back at the camera.

Outside, people have seen—and snapped pictures of—strange, filmy objects near a caboose on display. People familiar with the haunting suggest that if you look at the pictures closely, you can see the image of railroad workers of long ago.

Skeptics discount all the photographic evidence. They say that these photographs have probably been manipulated using double-exposure techniques; however, believers counter that many of these pictures were taken and developed when the double exposure technique was not a common practice and required technical know-how that was out of the reach of most photographers.

But, for believers, the ghosts of Hawaii's most haunted railroad museum show them that nothing—not even walls of water—can ever wash away the power and presence of these railroad spirits.

Of History, Heritage, and Hauntings

Brunswick, Maryland

In 1890, Brunswick, Maryland rested on the banks of the Potomac River, just a sleepy village on the Maryland-Virginia border. But the Baltimore & Ohio Railroad had plans to wake up this little community. The company began to construct a railyard in Brunswick, which would attract workers from all over the country. In no time, the town's population exploded to 5,000 residents.

Along with it, Brunswick residents noted a rapid increase in another demographic: ghosts.

According to longtime Brunswick townspeople and visitors, along with paranormal investigators, who were called in to check out the haunted happenings, the energy generated by bustling railroad activity may explain at least some of the town's paranormal activity.

One of the current centers of the town's supernatural phenomena, for example, is the Brunswick Heritage Museum, which is a nod to the town's railroad past and a structural testament to how that industry's influence shaped the community's history. For paranormal researchers who favor the haunted objects theory—that objects of the past can carry, attract, or even stir up paranormal activity—the museum is a treasure trove of investigative possibilities. The museum contains objects from the turn of the twentieth century, an era when the railroad began to dominate the community's economic and cultural life.

Some of the stories of the haunted activity at the museum include accounts that the spirit of a woman in a white dress can be seen on the second floor. The second floor is dedicated to the railroad's influence on the town's heritage, according to museum officials. Some people speculate that if the apparition is seen predominantly on the second floor, it's likely that the ghost is somehow connected to the railroad exhibit.

But there are other reminders that supernatural powers are at work in the museum. People familiar with the haunting say strange noises and voices are heard throughout the building. They are often heard when the museum is supposed to be closed, too, which might rule out that the noises are from living workers or visitors unexpectedly wandering around the halls and rooms of the building.

This hasn't gone unnoticed by the area's paranormal researchers who use the site as a haunted hunting ground. Over the years, and particularly in the last few years as the ghost-hunting rage began to explode, teams have gathered evidence—personal accounts, along with video and audio files—of the spirits that seem to reside in the heritage museum.

According to a Washington, DC–based NBC affiliate's report, a team of paranormal researchers from the Mason Dixon Paranormal Society conducted an investigation of the museum using an array of audio and video devices that they spread out at various points in the building. When the researchers checked out the video footage that they had gathered, they were disappointed. No spooky images or anomalous activity showed up. But, investigators said the audio recordings turned out to be a treasure trove of evidence that supernatural forces were at work in the heritage museum. In fact, they collected fourteen audio artifacts, or EVPs. One file in particular drew the team's attention. During the EVP session, a few team members heard a strange noise and began to move objects around, hoping to locate the source of the sound.

When they reviewed the tapes from that incident, they heard a voice distinctly say, "That's mine." After that, the voice began to laugh.

The investigators also marked some other sections of the recordings as possible EVPs. The team members said when they reviewed the tapes at various points in the investigation they could hear what sounded like human voices, although these instances were not as clear as the "that's mine" EVP.

Based on their initial results, the society's members were not ready to conclude that the museum was absolutely haunted. That would require additional follow-ups, paranormal investigator Darryl Keller told the television station.

"There is definitely something going on here," Keller said. "It might take us two or three more investigations to see or possibly capture something."

Another group of paranormal investigators from Maryland Paranormal Research reported that they captured weird audio clips and experienced wild electromagnetic spikes in certain displays during a 2013 investigation of the museum. The team added another strange incident that happened during their investigation to the pile of evidence collected that night. They said that the third floor of the building used to be a speakeasy. Before thirsty patrons could enter, they pressed a secret buzzer to gain access to the club. During the investigation, investigators said that buzzer inexplicably activated.

"There was no one on the floor at the time," the organization's blog states.

Going Deeper

Despite all the great evidence collected at the museum, experts suggest it's hard to say who is haunting the building and hard to determine the role of the railroad on the spooky activity there. In fact, there's at least one other legend that indicates trains and railroad men have nothing to do with the museum's paranormal activity. The source of the haunting may lie even deeper in the region's history, well before the days that marked the railroad era.

The museum allegedly is built on Native American burial ground, which is causing the weird activity, theorists state. And, according the *Maryland Paranormal* blog, the museum is headquartered in what was once an early twentieth-century building that housed a drinking society called the Improved Order of Red Men, which couldn't have gone over very well with the spirits of Native Americans. The EMF spikes that the Maryland Paranormal Research group recorded, by the way, occurred at the Improved Order of Red Men display.

Railroad Ghosts or Not?

The debate on who, or what, is haunting the Brunswick Heritage Museum will likely continue. It's basically divided into three camps. Some say Brunswick's railroad history has inspired the building's ghostlore. Others back the idea that the ghosts come from well before the railroad and white settlers ever arrived in Maryland. Another group has a more expansive theory: it's all of the above. Like every good educational institution, the Brunswick Heritage Museum has an open door policy for spirits. Ghosts of railroad workers, Native Americans, and townspeople who have passed on are welcome to come in and connect with other visitors and staff. Isn't that what heritage is all about?

National Railroad Museum Features a Five-Star Haunting

Green Bay, Wisconsin

In 1956, a group of concerned citizens dedicated to preserving the memory of the country's railroad past got together to create a national railroad museum.

It took a couple of years and a joint resolution of Congress, but the group finally got their wish. The result of their creativity, hard work, and political string-pulling is the National Railroad Museum, a Green Bay tourist attraction that introduces more than 100,000 visitors a year to the fascinating history of the railroad in the United States. According to numerous eyewitness accounts and stacks of reports from paranormal investigators, the museum introduces visitors to more than just how the railroad shaped American history. It introduces many of them to America's railroad ghosts.

One of the more prestigious ghosts in haunted railroad history may march through the halls of this museum. Reports from staff members, visitors, and even paranormal investigators suggest that the spirit of former President of the United States and five-star General Dwight D. Eisenhower haunts the building.

The haunting appears to be connected to one display in particular. In a real coup for the museum officials, an engine and two train cars—called Bayonet and Bayonet II—that once served as Eisenhower's mobile headquarters-on-rails were moved to the National Railroad Museum. The train played a role in some of Ike's most emotionally intense moments of the war. As the architect for D-Day, the seaborne invasion of France, Eisenhower rode the train throughout England so that he could visit the troops that would, at his command, fight and die on the beaches of Normandy. He also used the train for meetings with commanders and political leaders.

It's that emotional intensity that may have initiated the supernatural activity. This power became etched into the very fibers of Eisenhower's railroad war room and manifests in paranormal activity, witnesses say.

In one story, a volunteer was cleaning Bayonet II right before lunchtime. He decided he could finish vacuuming the rest of the car after lunch; he turned the sweeper off but didn't unplug it, and locked the car up. When the worker came back from lunch, he noticed that someone had not only unplugged the sweeper but had carefully coiled the cord back up. Weirder still, the vacuum was moved down the car, far from where he had last used it. He also noticed that if someone had pushed the vacuum, they made sure it didn't leave any track marks. Allegedly, Eisenhower detested the sight of vacuum cleaner track marks on the carpet. He would hand brush the track marks out!

Of course, the worker assumed another volunteer had helped him with the chore, but he polled everyone on the crew and no one had even entered the car, let alone cleaned it. And certainly no one had hand brushed the track marks from the carpet. The volunteer later found out that he had the only key to the car, and he was sure he had locked it before leaving for lunch.

Lots of volunteers believe the helper was none other than the spirit of General Eisenhower, who apparently has retained some quirky neat-nick tendencies left over from his days at West Point and in the army.

The display, of course, has become one of the must-investigate places in the museum for paranormal research teams. One group, the Midwestern Paranormal Investigative Network, added some of the video and audio evidence they collected to YouTube.

During an EVP session, the phrase "in the water," came up several times, which could be a reference to the D-Day invasion.

A ghost hunter for Fox Valley Ghost Hunters, who explored the museum in 2015, reported that their investigation also encountered some of these phenomena on board the Eisenhower display. One investigator claimed an unseen force pushed the team member aside in an aisle of the car. Footsteps could then be heard traveling down the aisle. Investigators also claimed to hear screams that seemed to echo from the distance.

Locked In

Staff members and volunteers also report encounters that are more terrifying than phantom janitors. Some workers told investigators from the Midwestern Paranormal Investigative Network that while going about their duties, some unexplained force locked them in cars that are on display in the museum. Imagine the fear they felt when they entered the car, thinking they were just going about routine business, and then hearing the door slam and the loud click of the lock as it slipped into place.

Fortunately, help was close by, but for a few harrowing moments, they had no idea how long it would be until they would be able to leave the car—or if they would leave at all!

In other cases, workers described the activity as more benign, but no less creepy. A few staff members stepped forward and said that, at times, they felt they were gripped by invisible hands. At least one visitor reported that she felt something, like a feather, or a few strands of hair, had touched her face.

In most cases, these phenomena have been verified by the paranormal investigators brought in to document the haunting. They experienced a lot of similar activity that the staff members had encountered—unexplained sensations and sounds—but the investigators are trained to debunk the supernatural events. However, despite efforts to explain the activity away, many ghost hunters have come to the conclusion that the place is haunted.

In an online report prepared by the Midwestern Paranormal Investigative Network, the team puts it obviously and succinctly: "From the evidence gathered during this investigation, it is of the opinion of the Midwestern Paranormal Investigative Network that the National Railroad Museum is highly active in paranormal activity."

Georgia State Railroad Museum

Savannah, Georgia

Now a tourist attraction in the peaceful city of Savannah, Georgia, the Georgia State Railroad Museum has historically been the hub of attention—although, for most of its history, that attention was of the unwelcomed sort. Conflict and death continually swirled around the site where the museum now rests.

During the American Revolution, long before any building stood on what is now called Tricentennial Park, this section of the city became the focus of opposing forces during the Battle of Savannah, one of the Revolution's bloodiest battles. An unorganized attack by French and American troops on a well-entrenched group of British soldiers led to a veritable slaughter of the attacking troops. About 800 American and French troops were wounded or killed, far more than the fifty-five British listed as casualties.

In the American Civil War, waves of Union troops rushed to Savannah as part of Sherman's March to the Sea. The soldiers burned buildings, tore up railroad tracks, and destroyed railroad factories and facilities. The complex of buildings that now make up the museum and National Historical site would have made a perfect target for the invading troops. Curiously, like a calm eddy in a violently swirling sea, the site was spared.

The railroad turntable at the Georgia State Railroad Museum, circa 2017.

But the museum wasn't spared, paranormally speaking.

With its history soaked in revolutionary violence, along with the everyday danger and excitement of railroad work and travel, paranormal experts consider the buildings that once made up the nerve center of the proud Central of Georgia shops and terminal facilities to be one of the most haunted sites in one of the South's most haunted cities.

There are about five buildings left standing of the thirteen or so original railroad buildings, most of which are haunted by either spirits of the complex's railroad past, or by ghosts tied to the violence that once seem attached to the place like train wheels on a steel track.

Red Coat

Over the years, tales have spread of encounters with a most unlikely host at a railroad museum. According to these tales, while strolling around the grounds, witnesses see a man dressed in a British military uniform of the Revolutionary War, or a "Red Coat," as they are typically called. The witnesses wonder: "Why would a Revolutionary War reenactor be on the grounds of a train museum? Shouldn't he be dressed like an engineer, or a conductor, or even like one of the factory workers who labored in the plant?"

Then they see the figure slowly fade away, or completely disappear, and know that they did not stumble on a living-history participant dressed up like a British soldier; they saw the ghost of one of the soldiers who fought during the Battle of Savannah, hundreds of years in the past.

Paranormal Check

Another haunted hub in the Georgia State Railroad Museum is the Tender Frame Shop and Master Mechanics' Office. Workers once built the frames for steam engines there and the office section of the shop served as the business headquarters for the operation. While there are no published accounts of anyone seeing an apparition there, witnesses have recorded strange activity, like the one about the appearing—and disappearing—check. A staff member told one paranormal blogger that the chief financial officer of the museum saw a peculiar slip of paper on his desk. It was a check dated from the 1950s. CFOs are not known for their carelessness with checks and cash, so he immediately ducked out of his office to find out who had placed the check on his desk. No one confessed and, when he brought people in to see the check just a few seconds later, the check had disappeared.

Blacksmith Shop Haunts

One of the popular spots for visitors in the museum complex is the Blacksmith Shop. The display includes machinery and tools like the ones used by the workers who built and fixed locomotives on the site. More than a few staff members and guests suggest those workers still may be on the job. The growls and roars of machinery are sometimes heard issuing from behind the closed doors of the Blacksmith Shop. Voices—like workers barking out orders and updates—have also been reported. When people go in to check, the sounds and the voices instantly stop. Other witnesses claim to have seen an apparition of a black man in work clothes in the shop.

Print Shop

One final haunted hot spot in the complex is the Print Shop. It used to be the place where workers would print the forms that the administrators needed to run the complex enterprise. They also printed the company newsletter in the shop. The humming sounds of printing presses and other types of machinery are often heard coming from the shop. But, there's no one in the room—and there's certainly nobody using the facility to print documents.

Skeptics and Believers

About 40,000 people visit this railroad historical site each year, skeptics and believers alike. Skeptics have more than a few explanations for the ghostly sights and sounds. First, it's an old place and creaky floorboards and squeaky doors can play tricks on the imagination. Along with that, they add that the stories of violence can prime the mind for so-called paranormal encounters. These explanations, however, are not likely to dissuade the dozens of people who say they encountered real—not imagined—supernatural phenomena at the Georgia State Railroad Museum.

Restless Spirits in the Sleeping Quarters

Port Moody, British Columbia, Canada

A century ago the building that now serves as the Port Moody Station Museum rattled with the percussive footsteps of train travelers coming from and going to destinations all around Canada. People say you can still hear echoes of those footsteps from long ago—and maybe even see the spirits of those travelers.

In 1908, the Canadian Pacific Railroad built Port Moody Station as one of two stations for its passengers. The station also contained quarters for the station master, who both worked and lived there.

As the needs of railroad changed, the station moved and eventually closed. The Port Moody Heritage Society bought, moved, and restored the building so it could live on as a museum that explores the rich history—especially railroad history—of the region.

History, though, has a way of showing up in unexpected ways.

Reports come in from staff and visitors—and, eventually, paranormal investigators—that the station is filled with ghosts. The interior of the museum isn't the only haunted spot on the property. It turns out that the sleeper car on display next to the museum is, ironically, very restless.

Several witnesses have heard the thud of footsteps echoing down the halls and in the rooms of the building. Others have heard the whispers of an unseen entity. The voice whispers numbers, like "2655," or the word "tickets." Obviously, the ghostly whispers seem related to the museum's railroad past.

Photographs appear to capture some of the spooky activity too. Weird lights and orbs pop up in pictures, even though the photographers swear no lights were on when they snapped the pictures.

Some people have even more hair-raising encounters with the unknown at the museum, but these run-ins don't happen in the building; they occur in a sleeper car, the genuine piece of the railroad past that sits next to the building. In the 1920s, no mode of transportation could beat a ride on the Canadian Pacific Railroad sleeping car called the Venosta. Museum officials, with help from the West Coast Railway Association, restored the Venosta with its two sleeping quarters and a ladies' powder room. The restoration crew took great pains to outfit the powder room and the sleeping car with genuine accessories from the 1920s.

One of those accessories, apparently, is the spirit of a woman who remains attached to the Venosta. Although details are scant, people say that the ghost of the woman has been seen in the car.

The sheer number of experiences and rumors of experiences that spread about the Port Moody Station Museum caused several paranormal investigation groups to request a chance to prove that either the museum is haunted, or that it's completely ghost-free.

Executive Director Jim Millar took the challenge. He had his own brushes with possible supernatural activity while working at the museum that made him honestly wonder about the supernatural status of the property.

"I've had a few experiences with noises and things," Millar told a reporter from CBC News. "So I thought, why not have it checked out?"

One team—Northern Paranormal Investigations—jumped at the chance to investigate. The team has almost a decade of experience researching the unknown in a range of spaces and properties, including homes, places of business, historical and military businesses, and cemeteries. They spent a few nights using the latest technology—including devices meant to capture changes in temperature and variations in light-wave intensity—to document any instances of unexplained phenomena.

Of course, they really wanted a run-in with the ghost that allegedly haunted the sleeper car.

On the latter quest, the group said they came up short, but told reporters other evidence suggests something weird is definitely going on in the museum, and they wonder if this weirdness isn't some way related to the ghostly female presence seen on several occasions. When the team checked out the sleeping car, for example, they reported that their flashlights and cameras malfunctioned, turning on and off at random times. Could this be a sign that the ghost of a woman was trying to communicate with them?

The recording devices also picked up the sound of voices, but not the female spirit. In fact, the investigators concluded that the ghost of a man named "Peter" was trying to reach out.

There's another question that consumes this team of paranormal investigators, as well as others: Why is the museum haunted at all?

A few theories have surfaced. One of the best explanations is that the building itself isn't haunted, but some of the objects on display there might be. For example, a bell stored at the museum has a deadly history. Rescuers snatched the bell from a train that crashed in a lumber yard in 1913, killing five workers. The spirits may be attached to the bell, according to paranormal theorists.

On the other hand, ghosts that haunt the museum may be related to either the live-in station masters or their family members.

Of course, this doesn't have to be an either/or situation; there might be something to all these reasons. It could be that the onetime station house combines the residual power of the thousands of souls who visited the station with the active power of a haunted family home and equally haunted objects.

It's a combination that makes Port Moody an uber-haunted piece of railroad past and a window into the paranormal present.

— Chapter 4 —
HAUNTED STATIONS

In mythology and folklore, life is often likened to a journey. We arrive in this world from an uncertain origin and seem to forever trudge toward an equally uncertain destination. All that's placed in between—all of our thoughts and actions, triumphs and struggles—we call life. We even use terms like "our station in life." What better metaphor for life—this sacred spot between origin and destination—is the railroad station?

Is this metaphoric power the reason why, as you will read about in this chapter, railroad stations seem to attract so many spirits and specters, caught in their own journey between life and death?

It's an interesting theory, but according to some paranormal experts it's only one conjecture. Many people familiar with the ghosts that haunt railroad stations believe that it's not some type of mythological metaphor that stirs up ghost stories within the walls of these structures—it's the history of tragedies and triumphs that have occurred over the years. For decades, and in some cases more than a century, railroad stations served as a hub of life, and death, for communities scattered across the continent. They were spots where young parents, fresh from the maternity ward, waited for the arrival of the train that would carry the couples and their newborns back home, and places where distraught family and friends waited for the funeral train to arrive with their loved one's casket stowed away—a strange, but not completely unheard of, railroad cargo in days gone by. If the walls of railroad stations could only talk, what tales they would tell—tales of victory and defeat, sickness and health, war and peace, love and hate, wealth and poverty and, yes, life and death.

Some say these railroad stations still do tell these stories—in the form of hauntings.

In the next pages, you'll read about some of the most haunted examples of spooky spirit-filled stations. In Ogden, Utah, the ghost of a murder victim, along with the spirits of passengers and workers, may be behind rumors that one railroad station keeps such a busy paranormal schedule. In Nashville, a railroad station-turned-hotel has a few ghostly guests that staff blame on the building's former use as a passenger hub, particularly during World War II.

The haunted station isn't a uniquely American phenomenon, either. In the UK, specters drift into and around the subterranean rail stations that the British affectionately refer to as the Tube. Some of the spooks that haunt these stations don't just reflect the glory of England's railroad past, but also seem connected to the kingdom's darker history—its sometimes violent, tormented history.

We'll punch our ticket for these tales of terror now.

Was a Weird Specter Seen at a Train Yard Sent to Warn Workers, Residents?

Austin, Pennsylvania

In 1910, the workers at the Buffalo and Susquehanna Railroad saw a strange visitor walking along the tracks of their railyard near Austin, Pennsylvania. Tall and painfully thin, the bizarrely lanky figure was dressed all in black. The workers didn't hold it against the man that he liked black clothes. But they found how he acted "queer" and "spooky," which were words they used to describe his actions, according to both the *Honesdale Citizen* and *The Clinton County*—far more disturbing.

The man appeared suddenly, and then disappeared just as suddenly. Sometimes, workers found him hitching a ride in one of the passenger cars. Other times, they saw him just hanging out near the railroad tracks. Witnesses also watched the man run across cars and slither between them.

He didn't look like any of the town's residents and nobody had information of new—queer and spooky—employees working for the railroad company that primarily transported lumber from the area's rich forests to market.

Why, you might ask, didn't a group of strong railroad workers—usually not very permissive of interlopers in their place of work—grab the thin man and give him a stern warning to stay off railroad property?

According to the account that appeared in the *Honesdale Citizen*, the appearance of the man just freaked out these normally brave men. In fact, his presence seemed to stun them.

"The railroad men naturally felt uneasy or scared with a ghost riding their cars, and none of them attempted to put it off when they saw it crawling between and running over the cars," the *Honesdale Citizen* article stated.

This fear of approaching the strange man, it turns out, may have led to disaster, people later speculated.

As more encounters with the railyard's man-in-black piled up, a flood of reports eventually filtered into just about every home and business of hardworking Austin. Nobody could figure out who the stranger was, or where he had come from. Many in the town had an unsettling feeling, which they couldn't articulate, that the ghostly figure of the railyard might be trying to tell them something, even warn them about something.

The people of Austin would not be the only ones who connected tales of the appearance of a monster or ghost with misfortune. In fact, Fortean history is full of such cryptozoological foul winds blowing into communities right before disaster struck. The most obvious occurred decades later in a West Virginia town ironically named Point Pleasant. Between 1966 and 1967, people in Point Pleasant reported sightings of a huge (some described it as being seven feet tall) winged creature who issued ear-shattering shrieks, like some species of demonic bat. They called him Mothman.

Over the next few months, witnesses said they saw the creature on highways and in local lovers' lanes—and especially near an old chemical and munitions plant. More than 100 people said they saw it, leading to one of the world's leading paranormal and Fortean writers to travel to the small town to investigate. His findings became the classic book, *The Mothman Prophecies*, which later served loosely as the inspiration for a movie starring Richard Gere.

Just like the people of Austin, the citizens of Point Pleasant struggled to make sense of the visitations. Some believed that

Mothman could be a hybrid creature created when an experiment at the chemical plant went horribly awry. Others suggested that he might be the ghost of an old Native American chief whom early settlers had wronged. Only a few thought the beast might be some sort of winged prophet.

In 1967, the Silver Bridge—which spanned the Ohio River and connected Point Pleasant with Ohio—collapsed, killing forty-six people. Many townspeople were convinced that the figure so many residents had seen may have been more than a cryptozoological curiosity; it may have been a flying, shrieking omen.

On September 30, 1911, the workers of the Buffalo and Susquehanna Railroad and the townspeople of Austin received a terrible reply to their questions about why the creepy visitor had haunted their town. Known in regional history as the "Austin Horror," a dam—one that had long caused worries in the town—that stretched across Freeman Run and helped power the Bayless Pulp & Paper Mill finally gave way. The rush of water and debris first destroyed the mill and then rushed downstream into Austin, destroying much of the community. When the wave finally subsided, rescuers found the town littered with smashed houses and buildings, automobile tires, and pieces of railroad equipment, most likely from the railyard the weird black-clad creature seemed to frantically investigate. When officials finally did a death count, they said the death toll was somewhere in the seventies, but other unofficial accounts put the number of deaths at eighty-eight.

The article suggested that one of Austin's newspaper reporters, perhaps acting on a tip from the railyard's man-in-black, escaped the calamity in time to give warning. He had recently discussed the apparition with people in the nearby town of Lock Haven.

"The man who brought tales of the apparition to Lock Haven, when the giant dressed in black was doing the ghost walk in Austin, figured prominently in the stories of the flood, as he was one of the many heroes of the disaster. He was a newspaper man and by good luck happened to be at home when the dam broke and sent out first news of the catastrophe, which was well written, considering the situation and the fearful story to tell the outside world," the newspaper stated.

While reporters filed into the town to write about the tragedy, the townspeople, too beleaguered by the disaster and its aftermath, failed to mention the ghost to the journalists.

"Everybody who escaped death in the flood had a sad tale to tell the correspondents, but none of them mentioned the ghost," the newspaper article continued. "If they did, one of the clever fellows might have begun his story of the flood with a ghost coming to Austin and being a spirit from the other side of life that came to warn the people of their danger and what was to follow; and that nobody cared to quiz the spook. The writer might have started his big news story truthfully. Who knows?"

Occult theorists are split on what the railroad prophet represents. As mentioned, he may have been a Mothmanesque creature who wanted to warn people about the impending disaster. There are others who suggest people didn't see a monster, but a ghost. Devastating fires swept through the railroad shops on at least two occasions. There are no official reports of casualties, but if there were, it could certainly be fodder for ghost stories.

The last theory is perhaps the most intriguing. Reports of the man-in-black—abnormally tall and skinny—match up with paranormal tales of the Slenderman. The Slenderman recently appeared in pop culture, seemingly without pretext. However, within a few years, drawings and computer graphics of the scare-crow-like creature began to spread virally across the internet. People then claimed they actually saw Slenderman, and two disturbed girls even tried to murder a friend as a sacrifice to him. Those familiar with Tibetan mysticism cannot help but see the connection between Slenderman and a tulpa, which is a mind-generated spirit first described to westerners by mystic and adventurer Alexandra David-Neel. She wrote that by concentrating on a mental representation of a monk, she—and others—later saw the monk appear in real life.

Now, to transfer this theory to the railroad visitor, we have to realize that a year before the flood that destroyed Austin, just as this weird spirit began to show up, the dam nearly burst following a rainstorm. In fact, after the near rupture, some say the dam actually shifted downstream a bit. The event terrified the townspeople. Could that combined fear generate enough psychic energy to produce a tulpa, in this case, the slender railyard monster? Was it a warning from the collective consciousness?

It's hard to answer, but according to most reports, we do know that after the disaster the strange man was never seen in Austin again.

Civil War Spirits Haunt Gettysburg Engine House

Gettysburg, Pennsylvania

By most measures, the railroad shop, normally referred to as the Gettysburg Engine House, shouldn't be haunted. After all, it's a fairly new construction (built in 1991) compared to most haunted structures in Gettysburg. And it doesn't look haunted. It's just a common, practical metal building. When most of us think about haunted houses or paranormally active buildings, we think of abandoned mansions, or old factories leftover from a bygone era. Gettysburg has plenty of those types of structures.

According to ghost hunting teams that have investigated the engine house, its spooky reputation is earned through the primary law of haunted real estate: location, location, location. Situated near where the bloody fighting that broke out on the first day of the Gettysburg battle, the building may be attracting spirits who perished during the fight and who may be buried on the grounds, according to these paranormal theorists.

Since the engine house is on private property, not many people have had the chance to witness first-hand the spirit activity in the facility. However, Mark Nesbitt, paranormal researcher and the most highly regarded author on Gettysburg's supernatural legacy, is one of the few who has been allowed to investigate the engine house. On one two-hour investigation, Nesbitt wrote in *Civil War Ghost Trails: Stories from America's Most Haunted Battlefields* that he turned a few skeptics into believers with the electronic voice phenomena he collected from that ghost hunt.

One spirit, whom Nesbitt said was named "Em," spoke so loudly that it distorted the recording. In fact, she spoke so loudly that Nesbitt did what most paranormal investigators would never request from a ghost: he asked her to speak more softly.

Several stunned skeptics listened as Nesbitt played the recording and they plainly heard a voice say, "I'll be quiet." The voice did not sound like anyone else on the team.

On several other occasions, the author and his team saw unseen forces kick a barrel off a tire and heard the sound of footsteps. In most haunted spots, these footsteps—a type of haunting referred to as an aural haunting—last a few seconds, just a few taps and a couple of squeaks. But Nesbitt said that whatever spirit was walking around in the engine house was putting in some serious paces. The distinct sounds lasted for about eight minutes.

Nesbitt and other paranormal researchers have come in contact with a few female spirits. Some suggest that ghosts of railroad workers and train passengers may be among the many spirits that haunt the property.

The *Ghost Adventures* crew—who visited the battlefield on the anniversary of the first day of battle—also checked out the area near the Engine House. They heard stories that a bunch of shadows could be seen walking along the ridge line at night. Another witness, a ghost hunter who investigated the Engine House, claimed that soldiers—Union and Confederate—have been seen in the building and also among the railroad cars inside and outside of the structure.

One legend suggests one possible reason the Engine House is so active, despite being constructed long after the battle. According to the story, when construction crews were digging a railroad cut through the terrain they found dozens of skulls, which may have been remnants of unmarked graves. The disturbed graves may have unleashed a torrent of supernatural energy, leading to these spirit encounters.

Of course, the restless spirits of the railroad workers and passengers seem to be pretty easy to explain too. With all the thousands, or maybe tens or hundreds of thousands of souls who passed by the hauntingly beautiful fields and ridges of Gettysburg, more than a few must have gotten attached. Really attached.

Tracking Ogden's Historic Railroad Past and Its Haunted Present

Ogden, Utah

Frank Yentzer went to work at the Ogden Union Station on the day before Valentine's Day in 1923 just as he had done so many times before. Little did he know that a deadly confluence of mistakes, greed, and just plain bad luck would send his world crumbling down on him. The results, paranormal researchers say, would echo into eternity.

This view is of the north-facing entrance of the Ogden arsenal's locomotive repair shop.

Ogden Union Station, or just Union Station, at one time served as the hub between the Union Pacific and Central Pacific railroads. As such, the busy station buzzed with passengers and railroad workers. To handle the influx of tourists and business travelers, the railroad companies constructed an impressive depot that featured a thirty-three-room hotel, restaurant, and even a barber shop. A majestic clocktower—an important reminder that railroads ran not on steam and steel, but on time—silently stood watch over the operation. Time, though, eventually took its toll on the operation. New forms of transportation to tote passengers and freight cooled the railroad economy. In 1923, a fire broke out in one of the hotel rooms, nearly gutting the place. Remarkably, even as citizens begged the company to raze what was left in the building and construct a new facility, the company insisted that work go on. Even as they contemplated their next move, a horrible accident forced their hand.

While Yentzer toiled away, a stone in the fire-damaged clock tower broke loose and fell right on an industrious worker, killing him instantly.

Facing criticism and increased scrutiny, the company immediately decided to replace the building, but according to paranormal investigators and folklorists, a piece of the past and that tragedy—Frank Yentzer—remains. There are those who say he can still be seen in the lobby of the building, toiling away.

An Ongoing Investigation

Jennifer Jones, an expert on the folklore and hauntings of the Ogden area and writer of the *Dead History* blog, has conducted numerous investigations of the paranormal activity going on at Union Station. She likes investigating the building because, first, a lot of the history that's discussed in the haunting is factual and, second, it's full of surprises.

"The Union Station is one of those buildings that seems to be hot or cold paranormally speaking," Jones wrote in an email. "When it's active, it's pretty active."

Over the years, Jones has seen shadow figures, experienced a range of paranormal encounters, and collected some compelling EVPs while investigating Union Station.

According to Jones, the most haunted spot in Union Station seems to be what's now called the Browning Theater, but used to be the mailroom when the building served as a train station and depot. She added that the spirits there seem to be playful, or more accurately, the spirits there like to toy with people.

"You would hear an odd noise on the other end of the building, head down that way, and then you would hear the same noise from where you had just been," Jones wrote. "We captured EVPs of what sounded like children and also women."

She believes that the theater is so haunted because of its use as a hospital and morgue after a railroad disaster, which will be discussed shortly.

"My team captured EVPs of what sounded like children on the stage in the theater and I have to think it's connected to that train wreck," she wrote. "There was an entire family killed in the accident, including two young girls."

It's pretty common to hear the sounds of footsteps pounding up and down the floor where the train platform once sat, too, Jones added.

Yahudi

Ghosts are also suspected in the conspicuous elevator rides that happen in the building. Suzan Crawford, a former Union State museum worker, told the *Deseret News* that her employees—

especially the ones who work during the night—told her they have seen the elevator go up or down and, when the door opens, there's no one onboard. Likewise, they've watched, mystified, as some force opens and closes a window.

In one of the more mystifying acts, Crawford reported, the window in the grand lobby was forced open, but nobody could figure out who opened it. The window is situated far above the ground, far above the height of the workers. To open it, a person would likely need a ladder. In fact, it was so difficult to reach that the mysteriously opened window remained untouched for a few weeks until—just as mysteriously—someone closed it.

That someone could have been the spirit of Yentzer, some paranormal theorists speculate. But the ghost of the unlucky accident victim isn't the only spirit that gets the blame. It might be a mischievous spirit that people-in-the-know call "Yahudi," or, to his friends, just plain Hoody.

Why So Haunted?

Frank, Yahudi, and a bunch of other spirits are just some of the many ghosts that haunt the building, which now serves as a local history museum—and actually it contains a couple of museums, including the Utah State Railroad Museum, the Eccles Rail Center, the John M. Browning Firearms Museum, Utah Cowboy and Western Heritage Museum, and the Browning-Kimball Classic Car Museum.

According to Jones, the thing that makes investigating the building so interesting is its varied history.

As mentioned, some of the haunted activity in the building may be related to its use as a makeshift morgue following a horrific train accident.

"There was a bad train wreck just outside of Ogden and they brought the dead and injured back to the mailroom as like a triage station," Jones wrote. "The living were moved on to the hospital and the dead were left there until they could be transported to local funeral homes and have families notified."

The shadow figure—and some of the other haunted happenings—might be related to a suicide victim.

"I tend to think that the ghost that is often seen there as a shadow figure is a man who killed himself in what was the mailroom back in the day, I can't remember the exact year offhand," Jones wrote. "I have seen this shadow figure myself and it was on the train platform, which is now an enclosed breezeway. It connects right to the theater."

Bloody Luggage

There's another reason that the station might be haunted. And this could possibly be the saddest, weirdest reason for a haunting ever.

According to Jones, a grisly discovery may have sent the supernatural activity in Union Station down the express tracks.

It all started on March 19, 1924. Alexander Brown served as a baggage handler and electrician at Union Station, which handled tons of mail and cargo that moved through the busy station. Brown noticed something weird about a trunk that he was loading into the train. As he packed the trunk on the train, he decided to tie an Airedale Terrier to the trunk. A soldier was transferring the terrier to his new base in Denver, according to the story. The dog, however, reacted strongly against his travel accommodations. He began to howl and growl at the big trunk.

The dog only calmed down when the handlers moved him away from the trunk.

Then, when he tried to move a big trunk, the package handler slipped. Brown examined why he almost fell. A small, dark pool of fluid coagulated at his feet. When he bent down for a closer look, he realized the substance was blood and it appeared to be leaking from the trunk.

Brown immediately called for a railroad investigator who quickly showed up on the scene.

When the inspector came and opened the trunk, they found the body of a woman, wrapped in two carpets. They noted that the woman had suffered head injuries.

Detectives investigating the case found bogus names and addresses were used for the shipment of the trunk from Denver. But a few witnesses stepped forward and identified the man who was conspicuously dragging the trunk through the streets of Denver—Fred Janssen. He was arrested and eventually confessed to killing his wife.

Ogden Exchange Building

Another railroad-related paranormal hotspot in Ogden is the Ogden Exchange Building. Jones points out that the Ogden Exchange Building housed railroad offices, as well as work spaces for employees who worked at the nearby stockyards.

Over the years, it's gained a reputation as one of the most haunted places in the city, but its recent use as a haunted house adventure site seems to have blurred folklore, storytelling, and actual paranormal encounters.

For example, several paranormal research teams have investigated the place and say they've collected decent evidence to back up the rumor that something truly anomalous is going on in the Exchange Building.

The *Deseret News* reported that one team videoed "mist and shadowy figures" traipsing through the halls of the building. They also used digital recorders to collect electronic voice phenomena—or EVPs—which are voices and noises that people typically can't hear during the investigation, but can be heard among the static and white noise of a sound file.

Billy Shields, an investigator for the Salt Lake Ghost Hunters Society, told the newspaper that one of the most convincing EVPs came during an investigation of the Exchange Building. Late at night, while he reviewed the files they recorded during the investigation, he didn't pick up a voice, or strange noise, actually. He heard a song.

"While I was listening to the tape, I distinctly heard a little girl singing 'Ring Around the Rosie,'" said Shields. "That's pretty creepy when you're sitting at your desk late at night, all alone." He paused and laughed. "But I suppose if you're going to listen to the ramblings of a ghost, there is no better time than late at night."

While paranormal research groups believe there does seem to be something weird happening in the Exchange Building, Jones isn't so sure. The building's use in the haunted house entertainment industry might be unwittingly leading to the confusion of fact and fiction. For example, the hauntings are often linked to two incidents, said Jones, and both of them are either untrue, or are based on faulty information. A triple homicide at the Exchange Building is often given as the reason why paranormal occurrences happen at the building. But that doesn't seem to be true. At least two people died of natural causes in the building and body parts from a homicide were discovered near the site, but no murders were ever reported in the building.

Jones also adds that, while the building did serve as a community mental health and addiction treatment center, it never served as an asylum for the mentally ill. A group of paranormal entrepreneurs cooked up that tale as part of their back story for a haunted house project they had staged at the Exchange Building. Unfortunately, it began to spread as a true piece of history.

But that doesn't seem to stop people from investigating and debating the once-proud piece of Ogden, Utah's railroad past.

Ghosts on the Waterfront

Vancouver, Canada

During the heyday of train travel and transportation, when money was streaming into the coffers of the world's railroad companies, railroad barons, these men of industry, did not spare any expense. Just look at the grandeur of Vancouver's Waterfront Station. A beautiful example of neoclassical architecture, the main building is framed with ionic columns and red brick. Millions of visitors, passengers, workers, and staff have stepped through this impressive depot.

The classic architecture must be exceptionally beautiful because not all of these people have left.

According to ghost hunters, Waterfront Station, built by the Canadian Pacific Railway, is among the most haunted places in Vancouver, Canada's jewel of the Northwest. And that's saying something because, as many experts on Canadian ghost stories point out, Vancouver is really haunted.

Waterfront Station, like so many other tales of haunted railroad, may have gathered much of its paranormal activity from its role as a travel and transportation hub. The people who came through these halls carried more than just their luggage: they also carried their stories and their problems. They toted their emotions and desires. They were also susceptible to deadly accidents and acts of violence. Paranormal theorists suggest that highly charged, emotional events can generate paranormal activity. If so, Waterfront Station qualifies.

One of those highly charged emotional events happened to a railroad brakeman working at the station, according to folklorists. They say that in 1928, the worker, known as Hub Clark, toiled in the yard, checking on the trains and the rails, while also making small repairs. There's no record of how it happened, but somehow the brakeman was decapitated. Now, people claim that a ghost—in the shape of a man without a head—can be seen wandering around the train tracks near the building. The odd specter holds a single lantern, they say.

While the headless brakeman is a standard bit of railroad ghostlore, other stories of spirits haunting Waterfront Station are harder to explain away as mere mythology. Many of these accounts come from security teams that patrol the station, often late at night or early in the morning. One guard reports that during his routine patrol of the west side of the building, he saw an unusual sight. As he peered down the dark, empty corridor, he saw the apparition of a woman, coiffed and attired in the fashion of the 1920s, dancing by herself. He didn't just see her dance. He said he could hear the music—much like the music from the '20s—that caused the ghostly figure to dance. As he moved in to get a better look, the woman suddenly disappeared and the music abruptly stopped.

Others have verified the nightwatchman's tale of sonic spookiness. Many have said that while they didn't see the dancing woman, they have heard the faint strands of music from a bygone era mentioned by the guard, even though the loudspeaker system doesn't play music.

Another guard tells a much different tale. He said that during his rounds he entered what he expected would be an empty room in the northwest corner of the building. But the room wasn't empty. A strange white glow pulsed in the room. Guards are used to chasing out vandals and keeping a watch out for burglars, but this night watchman was completely unprepared to confront this intruder. When the guard squinted his eyes and looked more closely, he saw the white glow emanated from the ghost of an old woman. The guard added that the woman wore a sad expression on her face.

His flight-or-fight response got stuck. He couldn't move, the guard later reported. He just stood in awe.

The ghost seemed to acknowledge the man's presence. She suddenly stood straight and then floated toward the guard. Now, his flight-or-fight response finally kicked in. And he wasn't about to fight a ghost. The guard turned and ran out of the room.

Another guard experienced a type of haunting that most parapsychologists would term either an intelligent haunting, or a poltergeist encounter. In one of the most frightening tales told about Waterfront Station's supposed haunting, the night watchman reported that he walked into a room used to store old desks. As he made his way into the center of the room, the desks seemed to take on a life of their own. The pieces of furniture moved around him, like they were trying to surround him.

The guard jumped onto one of the attacking desks and vaulted out of the room.

In a similar story, a night watchman, wielding his trusty flashlight, walked into a storage room in the basement. After a few minutes of fruitless searching for an item, he found himself deep within the cavernous room. He turned to exit. But his flashlight fell on an unexpected impediment—a wall of boxes. While he searched, someone had built a wall of boxes that stretched across the room, essentially walling him in the creepy, dark room.

I'll Come Back Another Time

In *Haunted Canada*, Joel Sutherland wrote that you don't have to wait until night to see a ghost at Waterfront Station—and some of these spirits apparently don't really care about your privacy. In one tale, an employee was chatting with a co-worker in the restroom.

Another woman approached the two and joined them. Neither of the ladies knew the woman and an awkward silence draped over the conversation. The witnesses noted that the woman had long wavy brown hair and seemed attired splendidly, but in an old-fashioned way.

After about ten seconds of silence, the woman said, in what was described as an ethereal way, "I'll come back another time."

And vanished.

Groups of Ghosts

It's not just the employees who see ghosts in Waterfront Station. For instance, travelers have seen other ghosts, and even groups of ghosts, while passing through the station. Tourists claimed they saw the spirits of three old women sitting on a bench.

And, finally, there are other hints that supernatural powers are punching their ticket at the transportation center. People hear hurried footsteps click-clacking along a tiled floor. But when they look around to find the source of the sound, no one's behind them.

It seems everyone is in a hurry in Waterfront Station, even the passengers trying to catch a train in the spirit world.

Tubes of Terror: The UK's Supernatural Subway System

United Kingdom

If you're in the United States, the best chance—or worst chance, for those of you who fear paranormal encounters—to run into a railroad ghost is to see one above ground—for example, along a solemn bridge, or at a lonely railroad crossing. But in the United Kingdom, a whole genre of ghost stories are buried just a few dozen feet below the roads and sidewalks of England's most populated cities.

England's storied subway system, or Tube, as it often called by Londoners, is apparently the most haunted place in the country. And that's saying a lot, because uber-spooky England is home to the world's most famous ghosts and the planet's most well-known haunted castles and manors. The interesting thing about the Tube ghosts, however, is that the stories aren't relegated to the past. New ones are cropping up all the time in the media and are spreading through various social media channels as you read this. We'll take a look at just a few of those tales of subterranean terror now.

South Kensington Station

The underground trains that snake under London are primarily utilitarian. They get you from point A to point B without the hassles of city traffic. But some people recognize the true architectural marvel and historical importance of the Tube, and these folks try to collect photographic and video mementos of their visits to the subway when they ride. And, sometimes, they get more than just mementos of architecture and history, they get evidence of the paranormal.

One rider in the Tube, standing in the Knightsbridge station, located in West London, decided to film his visit. He swept his smartphone's camera around the station, back and forth. As he did, he saw a flash of light in the dark tunnel. He reviewed the footage over and over again. He realized that it was no ordinary burst of anomalous electronic interference. The flash seemed to show a ghost lurking in the tunnel.

The witness later turned in the video to reporters, who immediately posted it online. The video went viral, landing on sites such as the UK's *Daily Star*.

According to some skeptics, the footage has an easy and natural explanation. Any bit of reflective material can be picked up by the smartphone's camera and anthropomorphized into the image of a man, or, in this case, a ghost. But believers suggest that the location of the sighting and the anomalous shape point to supernatural forces. They remind skeptics that this area was once an ancient burial pit. During the Great Plague of the 1600s, thousands of bodies were stacked there.

And that's led to more questions. Could this footage show one of those victims? Are there more lurking in these seemingly innocuous subway stations?

Bethnal Green

During World War II, as German Luftwaffe bombers and fighters prowled overhead, the English people, displaying the unique British ability to mix innovation with practicality, used the Tube not for transportation, necessarily—or for hunting ghosts—but they did use the city's extensive underground transportation system as an impromptu bomb shelter. And the Tube system held up pretty well for that use, too.

However, on March 3, 1943, the air raid siren sounded and thousands of Londoners filed orderly into the Bethnal Green Tube station. At first, everything went well, but, according to later reports, a mother and child fell down, leading to a chain reaction. Person after person fell as hundreds of others began to tumble. It quickly turned into a panic. By the time the situation was sorted out and emergency officials arrived on scene, 173 people—mostly women and children—had died, crushed and asphyxiated to death, medical reports indicated.

Echoes of one of the worst civilian disasters in England's World War II history continue to reverberate through the halls of the Tube station even today, according to several reports.

In one story, a worker said he was going through his end-of-night routine before he went home. He knew the last train had departed the station and all the passengers had gone with it. In fact, as far as he knew, all his coworkers were on their way home, too. He locked up and turned off the lights when he remembered he had a few bits of administrative work to finish. The man went back into the office. Suddenly, he was no longer sure he was alone.

The man claimed he heard children crying. But he kept working. However, the sobbing grew louder and louder. A few seconds later, he heard women screaming and the sounds of what he could best describe as the chaotic din of people panicking.

For fifteen minutes or so, the noises and phantom voices grew to a crescendo. Work ethic, or not, the man had had enough. He ran out of his office.

After consulting with his colleagues, the worker learned that he was by no means the only person who'd heard these strange noises, which most people took as ghostly echoes of the 1943 tragedy.

And, no doubt, he wouldn't be the last.

Liverpool Street Station

One Tube station in central London is considered another piece of the city's haunted Underground, but the origin of its spooky reputation may rest outside of the typical reasons, like accidents and murders, that ghosts lurk in London's subways. People say Liverpool Street Station's unique proximity to one of the most infamous institutions in English psychiatric history causes most of the supernatural activity there. They say that the station's location is so close to the Bethlem Royal Hospital that, every once in a while, a paranormal piece of the haunted site leaves the asylum grounds and takes a little stroll down the street to the station.

The Bethlem Royal Hospital, also known as the Bethlem lunatic asylum, is where we get the word "bedlam." And, apparently, bedlam is an apt descriptor of the goings-on at the hospital. Early on, the treatment of patients bordered on torture. Neighbors of the facility complained about hearing the screams and shricks erupting out of the facility. Then, there was the matter of burying the patients who died in the hospital—and there were thousands of poor souls. Staff members reportedly buried the corpses in what was basically the asylum's backyard.

Construction workers building the Liverpool Street Station reportedly came across some of those remains. And one way to stir up haunts is to disturb graves. If this didn't start the hauntings at Liverpool Street Station, paranormal theorists are convinced that, at the very least, it ratcheted up the activity.

One of Liverpool Street Station's most famous ghosts is the spirit of Rebecca Griffiths, a young woman who allegedly resided as a patient in the asylum. According to one legend, Rebecca was buried with her favorite coin in her hands. However, workers disturbed her grave during one of the construction projects for Liverpool Street Station. As a result, the coin slipped from her grasp. Now people claim to hear a horrific shriek that experts on the haunting say is Rebecca screaming in anguish as she attempts to find the missing coin.

And Rebecca has company.

In 2000, a worker monitoring the security camera feeds noticed something out of place. He saw a man wearing white overalls in the station. The station was supposed to be empty at that time, so the worker called the station supervisor, who decided to investigate. After a quick check, the supervisor radioed to his colleague that he couldn't find the man in overalls. The worker checked the cameras again and the figure in white overalls stood practically right next to his supervisor. The supervisor checked again and still couldn't see the intruder. Wisely, the supervisor decided to call off the search. On the way back to consult with the worker, however, the supervisor noticed something strange on the bench: a pair of white coveralls.

Maybe it was just a super-stealthy, super-quick human intruder. Or, it could be just another spirit permanently waiting for a ride in Liverpool Street Station.

Becontree Station

The Becontree Station is actually an above-ground station located in east London, but it's got such a reputation for paranormal activity—and features one of the creepiest tales in London's haunted lore—that leaving it out of this collection didn't seem right.

The station was built in 1932 and remained a calm hub for London's commuters, but the rumors that supernatural forces stalked the station began to spread after a horrific accident in 1958. Two trains collided immediately after leaving the Becontree Station, resulting in ten deaths.

After the accident, the busy but quiet station was never the same. People began to report strange occurrences soon after. Some of the reports are fairly standard in paranormal literature: noises and voices that issue from no visible source, objects that move on their own, and brief flashes of shapes and shadows at the edges of the witnesses' peripheral vision. However, one station supervisor had an encounter so brazen it stands out among the regular stories told about the paranormal in Becontree Station.

One night, the story goes, the supervisor settled in for his night shift. It's usually the quietest shift compared to the hustle and bustle of daylight commutes. But it's busier in other ways and in other dimensions. The supervisor said he busied himself in the office when the door rattled three distinct times. He checked—then double-checked—to see who was behind the interruption, but there was no one there. The platform, which the door faced, remained empty. An unsettling feeling washed over the man, who decided to take a break and walk to visit a colleague. After a nice chat, he walked down the platform, all the while feeling as if someone was walking behind him, or, to be more accurate, stalking him. He turned around and confronted a scene he would likely never forget. There, in front of him, stood a woman. He plainly saw that she wore a white dress and sported long blonde hair.

But, she had no face!

The supervisor stared for a few seconds, which seemed like hours, until the apparition faded away.

When he consulted his colleague, his co-worker reluctantly admitted that he, too, had seen the woman with the blank face.

People familiar with the haunting suggest that the account of the ghost of the faceless woman is a clue that the haunting of Becontree Station is related to that 1958 train collision. But skeptics say that the haunting has a more prosaic origin: tired people working long hours during the night may be susceptible to their overactive imaginations.

However, believers point to the Becontree Station not just as an example of real paranormal activity, but as evidence that—above ground or below—the rails around London carry more than just freight and passengers; they carry proof that the supernatural exists and it's not going away.

Union Station and the Ghost of Abigail

Nashville, Tennessee

If you stroll through the magnificent lobby and wander down the halls of the Union Station Hotel, gazing at the Italian marble, intricately carved wood, and cavernous ceilings, you can understand why someone might want to stay forever. And someone has.

According to guests and workers, along with folklorists and paranormal researchers, the Union Station Hotel has a visitor who checked in decades ago—and never left. They also think this long-term guest's stay is directly related to the hotel's past as a once-bustling railroad depot.

Believers suspect a few ghosts haunt the former Union Station, which was built in 1900 to become Music City's most important railroad station. It became a hub where fans arrived to visit country music's mecca, musicians departed for their national tours, and soldiers and sailors exchanged trains during the country's conflicts. All that passion, fear, and excitement translated into haunted activity, according to paranormal believers. They call one of those ghosts Abigail.

According to several sources, Abigail is the ghost of a young woman who haunted the railroad station and continues to prowl the hotel. While she's been seen in several spots around the hotel, she seems to like room 711 the most. Far from trying to exorcise that ghost, hotel staff say they try to make her feel right at home. The room has been decorated to suit her, according to hotel officials.

"It's meant to kind of be an homage to her," Kate Thompson, a sales and marketing director for the hotel, told a reporter from television station WKRN.

Hotel ghostlore states that Abigail was once the girlfriend of a soldier on his way to France to fight in World War II. She promised him that she would be right there, on the platform of Nashville's busy train station, when he came back. Good to her word,

Abigail stood on the platform waiting for her boyfriend when he was expected back from the war. But she received devastating news. Not long after her boyfriend sent her the word that he would be shipped back to the States, he was killed in action.

The Union Station in Nashville, Tennessee, circa 1900.

In a state of shock and grief, Abigail threw herself off the platform and into the path of an oncoming train. Abigail died instantly.

Thompson and other staff members at the hotel have experienced a range of paranormal phenomena and they've also listened to hundreds of visitors tell their own stories about encounters with Abigail, or whoever is haunting the hotel. For example, people hear the ringing of a phantom phone but they can't locate the source of the noise, and lights turn on and off by themselves. More troubling, random sounds erupt above the room too. The trouble with that is Room 711 is on the top floor: there shouldn't be anyone walking around on the roof.

Thompson told another guest's ghost story. She said that one guest who stayed in the haunted room heard the noises, but he was able to better identify the noises than most guests.

"We had a gentleman who was actually working for the company who stayed in this room and heard dragging noises above his head, and he said it sounded like furniture, like they were moving heavy pieces of furniture and just dragging it and dragging it," Thompson told the reporter.

It's more than just sounds. People see things—and people feel things.

On the seventh floor, especially, witnesses claim to see silhouettes drift down the halls, or catch shadows darting across the room from the corners of their eyes. Some folks even report the sensation that someone is in the room with them, or that an unseen presence is watching them.

First-Hand Account

Linda, a commenter on the *Ghostvillage* blog, corroborates much of what the staff and guests have experienced. The commenter stayed in the Union Station Hotel for a few days during a business conference. Initially, she was intrigued about the hotel's haunted reputation, even requesting a room on one of the "haunted" floors, but that interest would change as her stay wore on and the paranormal activity heated up.

Initially, at least for the first few days, nothing happened. The room seemed quiet and completely ghost-free.

On the fourth night, the exhausted business traveler decided to stay in while her colleagues hit the town. Like others who have experienced the Abigail haunting, the activity started with a "weird feeling," Linda wrote, adding that she felt "like I wasn't alone."

The feeling was so powerful that she turned on the TV and lamp and clutched the cordless phone, just in case she needed to call for help.

She began to drift off, eventually falling into a well-needed sleep. But a loud bang immediately woke her. She sat up but remained immobilized with fear.

The pounding exploded around her again.

Linda figured other guests would have heard the knockings too. Finally summoning the courage she needed, Linda walked across the room to the door and looked out the peephole into the hallway. She gazed on a quiet and empty hall. She turned to walk back to the bed when the knocking erupted again. This time, she just yelled, "Who is it?" but was met with a foreboding silence.

Linda called for security, who came to her room instantly. The officers told her they discovered nothing amiss and could find no natural explanation for the weird knocks. Linda stayed in bed, called her husband, and requested he talk to her until she finally fell asleep.

Her paranormal adventures, however, were just beginning. When she heard her husband snoring on the other end of the line, she knew she was on her own. In no time, the television suddenly clicked off, so she turned it back on.

Then the television and a lamp simultaneously switched off. Linda freaked out, ran to the bathroom, and switched on those lights. Still not wanting to admit paranormal forces were at work, she desperately tried to find the problem with the television and lamp. She found nothing out of the ordinary. There's reason to believe that Linda never heard about all of the supernatural phenomena others had experienced in the hotel, but the erratic light show was described in numerous encounters with Abigail.

She called maintenance and a man came to repair the light.

Linda mentioned the strange activity to the repairman. He told her he'd never seen a ghost, but he'd heard that others had experienced many of the effects—loud knocks, electrical device malfunction, etc.—that Linda had experienced. In a way, that made her feel good, but in a way, it scared her even more.

Linda did not experience any more paranormal activity during her stay, but she told the repairman before he left that her experiences made a lasting change. She believed that maybe Abigail sensed Linda's doubt and wanted to make her presence known.

"Then I told him I had requested this floor because I was told it was the most active, but I guess deep down I didn't really believe it," Linda wrote. "We laughed about it a little and I told him I certainly believe now and whoever or whatever it is can quit trying to prove it to me because I got it—point taken."

— Chapter 5 —

HAUNTED TUNNELS

The construction of railroad tunnels represents some of the most impressive architectural and engineering feats of their day. These passageways blasted through mountains and dipped under bodies of water to take passengers from here to there faster and more efficiently.

In spiritual and mythological symbolism, tunnels and caves represent something a little deeper. They represent a change in state. They can represent a change from the mundane to the magical and from the temporal to the eternal. For example, near-death experiencers say they encounter tunnels that lead them from their current reality to an afterlife state.

In the next stories, these two seemingly different structures—the railroad tunnel and the mythological tunnel—have more in common than you might have guessed. Railroad tunnels aren't just practical conduits to get people from point A to point B in the quickest way possible; in haunted railroad lore they are passageways into the paranormal.

To tour the first haunted railroad tunnel, we will revisit the haunted railroad capital, Altoona, Pennsylvania.

The Haunted Horseshoe Curve

Altoona, Pennsylvania

Above the city of Altoona, not too far from the Railroaders Memorial Museum, rests an architectural marvel that has served as an iconic landmark for the city and its historic connection to the railroad industry. The Horseshoe Curve is an achingly long 2,375-foot curve perched about 1,600 feet up in the majestic Allegheny Mountains.

The Curve isn't just noted because it's a prime example of railroad engineering, which it is. People also say it's a prime example of haunted railroad property. In fact, a couple locations at the historic site and near the historic site are considered haunted. For decades, people have told ghost stories about the tunnels at the Curve, but one in particular has resonated for generations.

This story starts with a young and beautiful Irish woman, one of the many railroader wives who married the men that labored to create the Horseshoe Curve. The work was hard and often dangerous. Each evening, according to one version of the legend, this young woman would head to the end of the tunnel and wait for her husband to walk through this long, dark, and empty tube. One evening, as the sun began to set over the Alleghenies that tower over the work site, she stood at the opening of the tunnel, but her husband didn't show up at the regular time.

She waited. And waited.

With each passing second she could feel panic and dread well up inside her. Finally, she saw a shadowy shape shuffling through the tunnel, heading toward the light. But when this figure appeared on the other side, it wasn't her husband. It was a company representative bearing horrible news: her husband had died in an accident.

A freight train pulling sixty cars is shown on the famous Horseshoe Curve in Pennsylvania, circa 1907.

Since then, people have claimed to see a woman dressed in a long white dress pacing outside the entrance to the tunnels that still remain near the Horseshoe Curve site. Some say she can even be summoned. In one technique, the ghost hunting hopeful is told to drive to the tunnel around midnight and then beep the car horn three times. Supposedly, people have seen a woman in a white dress appear and quickly fade away. Others say they've heard the voice of a woman. More ominously, there are those who said they saw nothing, but when they looked later, they saw handprints on their vehicle.

That's all pretty good ghostlore, right? And it's fairly typical for Pennsylvania ghostlore. Just up the road from this site, for example, people have claimed to have seen the ultimate example of ghostly folklore characters: the Woman in White, or the Lady of the Buckhorn. She is alleged to be the spirit of a car accident victim who appears to drivers daring to enter the forest after dark. But has anyone actually had a real run-in with this railroad widow?

Some say they've had encounters with the ghost of the tunnels, or at least experienced bizarre activity while investigating, or just visiting, the structures. A few commenters on *Discovery PA*, a blog dedicated to Pennsylvania travel, for instance, have left tantalizing clues that—ghostlore or not—something weird is definitely going on there.

One commenter wrote that she placed a recording device on the roof of her car. She waited for a few minutes but began to feel "very heavy" and left to analyze any evidence she collected. Later, while listening to the playback, she heard a "horrible growl."

"I still have that EVP and it still creeps me out," she wrote.

Another witness wrote that he and a group of friends heard either a group of children laughing, or a girl laughing, when they were in the tunnel.

The folks from JABA, whom we met in the story about the Railroaders Memorial Museum in Altoona, report they have had their own strange experiences in the haunted tunnel. In an email interview, John Albert said he and his JABA team had heard the rumors about the tunnel and decided to check on it themselves. He wrote that at about 10:00 p.m., he, his wife Beth, and a few friends made their way through the tunnel. About halfway through the tunnel, Beth, an empath who feels connected to the spirit world, stumbled backwards. John checked and saw no rocks or obstacles that could have tripped her. Beth thought one of her friends had tugged hard on her shirt. She said it felt like more than just a tug—the force of it pulled her back.

"She quickly realized there was no one behind her and those of us on her sides were not close enough to each other to have grabbed her shirt from behind, let alone be able to tug her enough to cause her to stumble," wrote John.

The investigators reported the experience was enough for them to not necessarily attribute all the activity to mere folklore.

"We had no other experience there, but to us, that was a credible paranormal incident," John wrote.

It's important to add here again that investigating or ghost hunting or just wandering around on railroad properties is dangerous and, in some cases, illegal. To stay safe and out of trouble, people are advised to tag along with an experienced team—they know where you should and shouldn't ghost hunt—and they should definitely get permission.

Tunnel of Terror— Sensabaugh Tunnel's Dark Past May Shed Light on Its Current Paranormal Popularity

Sensabaugh, Tennessee

Railroad ghosts are always on the move. This volume of haunted railroad stories offers several accounts of haunted railroad people and places that, somehow, can affect the surrounding community. Ghosts of train accident victims may wander away from the tragic site and inhabit nearby homes and communities, for example. Our next story is a little different. If the legend is to be believed, the ghosts that haunt this piece of haunted railroad real estate may be spirits of victims who were killed during a murderous rampage. However, that's just one of the legends buried deep in the dark, foreboding Sensabaugh Tunnel, one of Tennessee's great haunted railroad mysteries.

This mystery starts decades ago at a family home tucked into the crevices of a lonely country road that snakes through Sensabaugh Hollow, just north of Kingsport, Tennessee, on the Hawkins and Sullivan County lines. The date of the actual incident, if there actually was one, is hard to pinpoint exactly. According to the story, residents of this normally quiet section of the community woke up one morning to hear the dreadful news that the husband of a small family in the hollow went berserk and killed his whole family, including a baby. The wife, one grisly report suggested, held the baby in her arms as the bullets ripped into her flesh. Even at death, she refused to let her baby leave her arms.

That's the story, at least. But there are dozens of legends about the incident, including one tale where the husband was actually the hero, chasing after a kidnapper who took the baby through the woods and toward a stream, only to find that the madman had drowned the baby.

It's hard to say whether there is any truth to these stories. The years, memories, and fertile imagination seem to have painted over the facts, like the graffiti messages plastered on the walls of the Sensabaugh Tunnel. But the tunnel continues to yield new dimensions of the legend. According to locals, you might not be able to discover facts about the murder, but you can still hear the voices of the victims. Witnesses say they have heard a baby's cry echoing down the tunnel's walls. Voices and, even more frighteningly, screams, have been heard in the tunnel too.

Other people say they've even dared to summon the spirits. They have driven to the tunnel at night and turned off the headlights of their vehicle. The car begins to shake, an imperceptible vibration at first, but then the vehicle starts to rock, really rock. Believers say it's the spirits desperately trying to crawl their way into the safety of the car. In another twist of this tale, some witnesses claim that they've tried to restart their car after trying to contact the spirits and the engine refuses to turn over, at least initially.

So, is this all just some fun folk tales and ghostlore, wrapped into some adolescent fun?

Well, although not everyone can agree about the details behind the haunting, or even agree if there is a haunting, this has not stopped paranormal enthusiasts from investigating. One group, Knox Paranormal Researchers, released a few videos of their investigations into the alleged supernatural activity in the tunnel. Their conclusion offers a mixed bag of evidence into the authenticity of any phenomena at Sensabaugh Tunnels. For instance, they performed a car test to see if their vehicle would stall after shutting it off at the tunnel site; it fired right back up. They didn't observe or sense anything strange while in the tunnel, either.

The researchers were just about ready to call the tunnel investigation a bust when they discovered a weird bit of evidence. In another video posted by the investigators, the team offers one interesting bit of EVP. Paranormal researchers say that, often, the team's digital recording devices pick up noises and voices that are inaudible to them at the time of the recordings. In this case, the EVP seems to reveal the sound of a crying baby, echoing, just as legend has it, from the end of the tunnel.

Here's another bit of evidence that suggests the tunnel's reputation is more than just a flight of folkloric fancy. One night, close to Halloween, a freight train was barreling through the section of tracks near the Sensabaugh Tunnel when the engineer saw a woman on the tracks. Certain that the train hit her, he slammed on the brakes and brought the train, eventually, to a dead stop. The engineer shouted to the conductor to call the police and an ambulance. Police and rescue crews rushed to the scene to find a visibly shaken engineer. He described the woman as white and wearing a black shirt and white pants.

The rescuers scoured the area but never recovered a body.

Police had an easy answer for the incident: a bunch of jerky Halloween pranksters put a mannequin or scarecrow on the tracks.

Here's how the police report puts it: "Our town has had some vandalism over the past few days, including the taking of some of the scarecrows off the utility poles on Main Street. Some were found standing in and near the Sensabaugh Tunnel. We believe that, as a prank, one of the missing scarecrows was placed on the tracks to make the conductor think it was a real person."

Here's the thing, believers point out: the crews, who searched for the body and came up empty, also, allegedly, couldn't find a shred or a thread of evidence that even a scarecrow was used in the prank.

Cloaked in tales of murder and veiled in a mixture of true stories and flights of folklore, skeptics and believers alike will continue to dig into the stories of Sensabaugh Tunnel, trying to find the truth.

Flinderation and the Supernatural Railroad Nation

Salem, West Virginia

Tunnels are just creepy places, even the non-haunted ones.

They're dark, dirty, dusty, and dangerous. They have all the charm of a coal mine—without the mineral wealth.

Whether any of these thoughts drifted through the minds of the three-man railroad working gang tasked back in the day with repairing the tracks in the Flinderation Tunnel, also known as the Brandy Gap Tunnel, we'll never know. They didn't live long enough to tell us.

Most of the workers in the late eighteenth century and early nineteenth century knew how difficult and dangerous repairs in the tunnel could be, but few internalized just how quickly and silently death could be brought on. According to one legend about the haunted tunnel, the three workers laboring in the dank, 1,086-foot long tunnel near Salem, West Virginia, never heard the sound of an unscheduled train barreling down the tracks.

Only one worker, according to one version of the tale, cleared the tracks before the train hit him. But the other two workers didn't—and were killed instantly by the impact of the massive train engine.

And the Flinderation Tunnel—once a busy section of the B&O and CSX mainline—has been haunted ever since.

While it's hard to find any news stories about this accident, it's pretty easy to find stories about the haunting. There's a wide range of supernatural phenomena reported there. For example, some people claim to have seen the ghosts of the two workers, but others say they've witnessed a ghost train—complete with lights and roaring engine—dashing into the tunnel, perhaps in an eternal reenactment of the moment when the two workers met their ultimate fate. Still other witnesses say they haven't seen the ghost train, but they've heard it. The clank of a bell, the shrill scream of the whistle, and the hiss of the steam engine can be heard on some dark nights.

Paranormal investigators have collected what they consider evidence that some sort of railroad-related accident is causing the haunting. The investigators say they've examined digital audio files containing EVPs that they've collected at the site and could hear the unmistakable sounds of sobbing and ear-piercing screams.

Other people hear the pounding of feet coming toward them. Is it just their imagination, or the footsteps—perhaps of those workers trying desperately to outrun the train—echoing throughout eternity?

"Pushing Out of the Way"

One paranormal investigator writes about his investigation on the website Ghosts and Stories. He started his investigation at about 8:00 p.m. and came equipped with an arsenal of equipment to gather evidence about the haunting in the Flinderation Tunnel: digital recorder, laser thermometer, camera, camcorder, and trigger objects, which are objects from the past that might attract a ghost's interest. For example, a ghost hunter might use an old tool that the workers from the tunnel might have been familiar with, or a pocket watch that most railroaders kept on hand.

The ghost hunter began to ask questions about the accident out loud and, specifically, inquired what duties the men had when the tragedy struck. All the while, he made sure to switch on the digital recorder and camera, ready to collect any evidence.

He didn't have to wait long. The sound of footsteps walking past him caught his immediate attention. The investigator kept asking questions.

Without warning, a force pushed him to the tunnel wall.

He then asked, "What are you doing, trying to scare me?"

The answer came through the investigator's "Frank's Box," a device that gathers random bursts of words by sweeping through the AM radio frequency. It said, "No, pushing out of the way!"

Haunted tunnel believers would suggest that one of the spirits involved in the tunnel tragedy—perhaps even the ghost of the man who survived the incident—may have issued this strange warning. Some witnesses, for instance, have heard a voice shout, "Quit pushing!" and "Help me!" during visits to the tunnel.

Other Spectral Suspects

Not every expert on the Flinderation Tunnel believes the two dead railroad workers are the source of all the haunted activity going on at the site. The variety of ghostly tales seem to indicate another source, or, better yet, multiple sources for the activity. Some believe that the Ku Klux Klan held lynching parties near the tunnel and the ghosts seen here are sorrowful, or maybe vengeful, victims of those horrific crimes. There are some who suggest the top of the hill that the tunnel burrows into was once the site of a cemetery.

What makes the tales of railroad sounds and ghostly train lights even more suspicious is that crews tore up the tracks some time ago to help make the tunnel part of the popular North Bend Rail Trail.

But it might be that the trail isn't just popular with hikers and exercise fanatics. It might be popular with old railroad ghosts too.

—— Chapter 6 ——

HAUNTED TRACKS AND ACCIDENT SITES

When you have hundreds of tons of iron, steel, diesel and steam engines, passengers, and freight skating along two thin rails, bad things are bound to happen. And when they do, bad things happen in spectacular fashion. Railroad crashes have caused thousands of deaths, injuries, and general misery. According to some paranormal theorists, residual spirits remain anchored to those accident sites.

The railroad industry was also known for labor strife. Management battled workers, workers battled management, and often workers—worried about losing their jobs—battled their fellow workers. This tension led to violence, which led to injuries and death. And those deaths, witnesses say, led to ghosts.

In this section, we'll look at several haunted tales of ghosts and spirits that are connected to crash sites and scenes of unspeakable violence.

Eerie Echoes—The Return of the Red Arrow

Altoona, Pennsylvania

"People started screaming, and I braced myself against the windowsill," is how one survivor, a seventeen-year-old sailor at the time, described the sheer terror of the crash of the Red Arrow, a train barreling around the Bennington Curve, located between Gallitzin and Altoona, Pennsylvania, in the wee hours of the morning on February 18, 1947.

It's a scenic route. The Bennington Curve is near the highest point on the Pennsylvania Railroad in the Keystone State, according to author Dennis P. McIlnay.

"In Harrisburg, the railroad is only 310 feet above sea level, but by Altoona, the road rises to 1,174 feet above tide. In the next twelve miles, the railroad climbs almost one hundred feet per mile to nearly 2,200 feet above sea level at Bennington Curve," McIlnay writes in *The Wreck of the Red Arrow*.

Running behind schedule and trying to make up time, the train crew attempted to increase the speed of the train as it bended around the curve. Too fast, it turned out. The train jumped the track and several cars plummeted down an embankment, killing twenty-four and injuring more than a hundred.

The death and injuries deeply affected the community, but Altoona was no stranger to train wrecks. To this day, no one could have predicted just how deeply this derailment would cut into the very fiber of time and space of the accident site. The Bennington area soon became a hot spot of haunted happenings, and many who witnessed the frightening activity at that site blame that accident on a cold winter night back in 1947 for unleashing the paranormal outbreak. These witnesses now report that Bennington, which, at the time of the crash, was basically an abandoned worker's community that faded when the jobs left, is now a ghost town in more ways than one. And the population is reportedly booming.

According to the *Big Book of Pennsylvania Ghost Stories,* by Pennsylvania paranormal research legends Patty Wilson and Mark Nesbitt, the crash has generated some of the area's spookiest ghost stories. The duo wrote that eerie echoes of the crash still linger.

Witnesses in the Bennington area say that, often, usually on the anniversary of the crash, they are stunned to hear the sounds of screeching metal and the tremendous thud of thousands of pounds of passenger train cars leaving the tracks and twisting down the embankment. Then, the eeriest part of all—total silence. Seconds after the definite sounds of a train crash, witnesses say the mountain and the valley become completely quiet, like a spontaneous moment of prayer or silent meditation has been called. Obviously, when they go to investigate, there's no train wreck. And moments later, the area returns to normal.

Before you begin to brush off this as typical ghostlore, albeit super sad and creepy, Wilson blogs that some of these tales come from credible sources. She writes that two years after the wreck, a lineman, someone very familiar with the sounds of trains, heard the sounds of a crash—metallic crunches and earth-shaking thumps. He also heard screams of pain and fear. He ran to find the source of the sounds, but the area was completely deserted.

Then the silence followed, and he returned to work.

It was only later, once he had a chance to reflect on the incident, that he realized the day he had spent working near the Bennington Curve was the two-year anniversary of the crash.

The site has been supernaturally quiet lately, according to most accounts. But every once in a while, a new tale will crop up, often a slice of ghostlore that's passed from person to person, but some are also first-hand accounts written on a website. Here's one from the website *Ghosts of America*:

"We were driving down the road past the Red Arrow train track in the middle of the night, and about a hundred feet away we saw a floating train and shades covering the windows and behind those shades we saw figures... People... In a floating train... Bizarre! I never believed in the supernatural. We believe this is the train from the Red Arrow train wreck coming back."

Perhaps the Red Arrow hasn't quite reached its final stop.

Dead Railroad Men Do Tell Tales

Malvern, Pennsylvania

The world's haunted railroad stories that we are exploring in this book are often described as folklore. Ghostly brakemen, specters of accident victims, and even entire ghost trains are a kind of folk fiction that grew up and spread in a time before television, movies, and electronic media became the storytelling media of choice. In those days, people told stories as a form of entertainment and, often, education. This partially explains the popularity of railroad folk legends, like Casey Jones, and offers an explanation of some of the stories in this volume.

But you're making a mistake if you think that folklore explains all the stories, as the people of Malvern, Pennsylvania, recently learned. For decades, people ascribed reports of ghostly lights and spectral sightings on the railroad tracks near that site to a clever bit of railroad ghostlore. The ghost story indicated that the lights and ghostly experiences near the railroad tracks were tied to a bunch of railroad workers who died, or were killed, in Duffy's Cut, an area near those tracks.

Just a silly ghost story, skeptics said—until some people decided to actually investigate. Twin brothers Bill and Frank Watson told CNN that their grandfather, an executive assistant at the Pennsylvania Railroad, revisited a ghost story every Thanksgiving. Bill and Frank's granddad, who had kept the official files related to the haunting, told them that a man reported to officials that he saw the strangest sight during a walk by Duffy's Cut one warm September night—orbs of green and blue light dancing in the mist. The witness even made an official report, and he believed the dancing lights were the ghosts of a group of Irish railroad workers who died from cholera.

In the report, the witness said, "I saw with my own eyes, the ghosts of the Irishmen who died with the cholera a month ago, a-dancing around the big trench where they were buried; it's true, mister, it was awful."

The documents quote the unnamed man's description of the paranormal encounter, adding: "Why, they looked as if they were a kind of green and blue fire and they were a-hopping and bobbing on their graves ... I had heard the Irishmen were haunting the place because they were buried without the benefit of clergy."

While most people in the area thought of the ghost story as just a fanciful legend, the Watson brothers thought a true piece of history may have inspired the ghost tale and they decided to investigate. When their grandfather died, they inherited his papers. In the stacks and stacks of railroad reports, the brothers discovered clues to the origin of the haunting.

According to one account, the workers were buried in an area near where they were helping to build a railroad bridge. The brothers decided to start their own dig and quickly uncovered some evidence that suggested they were on the right path. The brothers discovered forks and a pipe, emblazoned with an Irish flag. Bill called that a "Holy Grail" and indicated they needed some help.

A geophysicist from the University of Pennsylvania joined the excavation. The scientist brought along technology that helped them scan the area so that they could search underground for evidence without digging or drilling. They discovered one area in particular that suggested something solid rested deep under the surface of the turf. After pinpointing this area, the team discovered an initial find—a human bone. But the mystery was just getting warmed up. As the team uncovered the remains of what appeared to be a mass grave, they began to wonder about the accuracy of one of the folktales. One legend that passed around the area indicated that the ghosts were not only victims of a cholera outbreak but they were also the victims of prejudice at the time that kept the Catholic workers from receiving proper care and treatment for cholera at local hospitals.

Now, this team suspected that the remains of the fifty-seven people—probably all members of an Irish railroad crew—exhumed from the mass grave offer evidence that some of the dead may be not just disease victims but murder victims. Skulls show indentations and holes that may be evidence of bullet holes or strikes from a hammer. The researchers suggest that residents may have murdered the cholera victims because they were afraid the disease might spread into their communities.

The lack of official records and the hasty mass burial also indicate that the railroad bosses and local officials wanted to quickly cover up the incident.

The ghosts of the workers, though, had other ideas.

Bodies Exhumed, Spirits Remain

Paranormal investigators say that even though the mystery has been solved and the stories of the workers' untimely end can be better known, supernatural activity at the site continues. Recently, facing a mixed reaction from the researchers who took part in the discovery, a group of paranormal researchers gained approval to conduct an investigation in the Duffy's Cut area. Some of the team that discovered the mass grave criticized the ghost hunting effort as unscientific, but they eventually relented and let members of the Chester County Paranormal Research Society—CCPRS—on the site of the massacre and allowed them to collect data, according to a story posted on the *Phantoms & Monsters* blog. In fact, two of the members of the team that found and excavated the site accompanied the investigators and even asked the spirits questions during the session.

The team used camera equipment with motion sensors and detectors that can measure the electromagnetic field. Paranormal theorists say that the electromagnetic field (EMF) detectors can sense slight changes in the electromagnetic field, which they suggest could be the energy of spirits. They also brought along a device, which was mentioned earlier, that scans the AM radio band and blurts out snippets of sounds and people talking, called Frank's Box, or the Ghost Box. Theorists also suggest that spirits can use this device to communicate with the living.

Early in the investigation, the team reported little interaction, but over the next few hours, as the night grew deeper, things heated up. They even had a purported conversation with the spirits, who expressed their anger at some of the parties that historians say played a role in the massacre. For example, a researcher asked whether the spirits knew "Duffy," obviously referring to Philip Duffy, an Irish contractor who had hired the men, and grew rich from the contract to build the section of railroad.

The spirits replied through the Frank's Box, "Yeah, the devil."

Another reply to the question "Are you with God?" revealed their current torment: "No… no… abyss."

Other paranormal buffs wonder whether the spirits that inhabit the massacre site are connected to some of the other supernatural activity that seems to envelope the town of Malvern. Some experts on the town's hauntings wonder whether the ghosts of Duffy's Cut aren't the spirits behind the haunted activity at a nearby inn, the General Warren. Homeowners of properties close to the site have also complained of anomalous events that they ascribe to the influence of Duffy's Cut's ghosts.

In many stories of the paranormal, ghosts want some form of justice before their spirits can rest. Despite the best efforts to settle the souls who were struck down in Duffy's Cut, it seems like the ghosts of these railroad workers are still restless and wandering.

The Legends of America's Most Haunted Railroad Crossing

San Antonio, Texas

For students, field trip day is one of the many highlights that dots the annual school calendar. Field trips allow students a chance to get out of the dreary confines of the classroom and see some of the sites. Win-win.

And spirits were still high for a busload of Catholic school students traveling back from a field trip that, according to locals, occurred sometime in the 1930s or 1940s near San Juan Mission. As some of the students talked and others snoozed in the back of the bus, the driver, a nun, carefully navigated the vehicle down Shane Road, just south of San Antonio, toward the railroad crossing. The bus lurched up the hump over the tracks and, just about halfway across the tracks, it suddenly stalled. The nun's eyes widened as she looked up the track; she saw a train light appear in the darkness of the evening and lock right on the bus. At first, she tried desperately to start the engine. Again and again, she twisted the key and revved the gas pedal, but nothing happened. She tried not to panic her students.

Because the nun wanted to avoid a panic, she did not attempt to open the door and help the students evacuate to safety. That decision would haunt her for an eternity.

As she turned the key one last time to start the bus, the light from the train engine and the shrill sound of its horn flooded the bus. The children saw the danger too late. The massive locomotive cut through the bus the way a bullet pierces the skin of an apple. All the children died. The nun was tossed through the windshield and survived.

A few weeks later, the nun drove to the crossing and waited for the next train. She saw one coming down the line, shifted the car into drive, and stopped in the middle of the track, waiting for the train to end her misery and guilt.

But then she heard noises: they sounded like voices of small children. She could hear what sounded like tiny hands pounding and tapping on the back of her car. Seconds later, just as her fate seemed sealed, she felt the car begin to drift forward. She looked out the window and into the rearview mirror in a fit of desperation, but the nun couldn't see anyone around. It seemed like an invisible force was moving her car. Mere seconds before the train would have hit her car and certainly ended her life, the vehicle slowly and effortlessly rolled off the tracks and into safety.

According to folklorists, this strange account contains the reason why the intersection of Villamain and Shane is haunted to this day.

But it's only one story that explains the bizarre phenomena that occur at the crossing. Like a lot of ghostlore, a bunch of variations are combined and subtly altered. Another tale, for instance, indicates that a nun wasn't behind the wheel of a bus; it was just a normal school bus crossing the tracks on its way to school when a train slammed into it.

While the details change, ever since the accident—or accidents—most people claim to have come into contact with the ghosts of these accident victims, and these encounters are among the most bizarre experiences in haunted railroad lore. People claim that they have heard the laughter of children and what sounds like small hands tapping on the back of their vehicle, just like the nun in the story. Some also report they have even felt their cars drift forward, like an invisible force was pushing their vehicles over the railroad crossing.

According to one legend that has been passed around the residents of the area, a skeptic went to the site with an ingenious experiment to either prove, or disprove, any supernatural phenomena at the railroad crossing. She drove to the railroad crossing and stopped. Then, she spread baby powder on the back of her car. When she put the car in neutral, she felt the car begin to drift over the railroad crossing. Seconds later, her car lurched safely to the other side. The witness then checked the baby powder and said she could see what looked like the swirl of palm and fingerprints embedded in the powder.

Cynics may scoff at the evidence—palm and finger patterns could be whipped up by the breeze of a moving car, for example —but at least the results of the experiment satisfied this now-former skeptic.

It's not just kid-powered cars and baby-powdered trunks that make people believe spirits are present on this stretch of tracks. Witnesses have heard and even seen ghosts in this spot, sometimes referred to as one of Texas's most paranormally active locales.

Some say they've heard the distinctive blast of a steam engine whistle, the rumble of wheels chugging down the line, and the grind of brakes attempting to slow the big machine. But, after a few minutes, no train ever passes and there's no sign of any engine, especially a steam engine, when they look up and down the line.

In another famous ghost tale told about Shane Road, a woman was driving toward the crossing at night. Her heart nearly stopped when she saw a little girl standing at the side of the road. *It's not safe walking at night on the road*, the woman instinctively thought. She pulled over and offered the girl a lift to her home. The girl climbed in and gave the driver directions to her home. *Perhaps the girl tried to run away from her parents*, the woman thought.

Once at the house, the woman told the girl to stay put and she would smooth things over with her parents. She started toward the house and decided, for some reason, to check on the girl.

When she looked back, the girl had vanished. But the woman had never heard the car door open or slam shut. The woman ran back toward the car and saw that the girl was nowhere to be found.

But the seatbelt was still buckled.

In another version of the tale, people say that the ghost of a little girl who carries a teddy bear haunts the railroad crossing. She even turns up in photos.

And other people have passed on accounts that the ghosts of the railroad crossing reveal themselves in even stranger ways. While one bird enthusiast drove a new pet parakeet home, she noticed something strange. The bird happily chirped and sang constantly from the moment it was placed in the convertible for the ride. Then, the witness slowed her car down to cross the track. The bird suddenly quit singing. For a spooky few seconds, the formerly chipper parakeet became dead silent, until they crossed the tracks and moved out of the area. Then the parakeet started to sing again.

We know that coal miners often used canaries to warn of impending mining disasters. Can parakeets somehow sense the paranormal forces that emanate from haunted railroad locales?

Historic Evidence?

As compelling as the story of the ill-fated bus and children ghost rescuers is, there's a problem with the tale. Nobody can find any evidence that a bus accident ever occurred at the crossing. One headline in the *San Antonio Express* from 1938 does detail the gruesome train-bus collision during a snowstorm that claimed the lives of several student passengers. But that occurred in Utah. Could that tale somehow have been mixed up with the Shane

Road legend? That's a possibility. Other theorists suggest that the tale is based on a car accident that occurred long, long in the past. Over the years, it morphed into the legend of the suicidal nun and the accident-prone field trippers.

That, however, is something for future debunkers—or believers—to investigate.

Spirit Photography Captures Eerie Signs of Haunted Railroad History

Hamilton, Ontario

On a cold, early February night in Ontario, George Brady, along with his wife Cathy and other members of the Hamilton Paranormal team, headed off toward their objective: the Sydenham Railroad Bridge, one of the most haunted spots in the Hamilton region, which is an area noted for the number of railroad sites that are rumored to have high levels of supernatural activity.

George reported on his organization's website that as they started toward the bridge, the beam of his teammate's flashlight swung toward the set of stairs that climbed the bridge.

George, who has seen a lot in his years as a paranormal investigator, couldn't believe his eyes. He saw the dark yet unmistakable shape of a man standing right outside the edge of the flashlight's circle of illumination. And it wasn't a shadow.

"The shadowy figure of the man was in an upright position, not on the ground like a shadow, and there was no other light source coming from behind us so it could not have been a trick of the light," George explained on his blog. "We did all agree that we could feel something in the area and knew this would be a good night in spite of the light snow."

As the beam of light swung toward the shadowy figure, the spirit—or whatever it was—walked away. Only George saw the shape, but the weird night was only just beginning and pretty much everyone on the investigation seemed to have an encounter. During the evening, the members would snap numerous pictures that revealed light anomalies, weird mists, and strange orbs. George and his team believe that the resulting treasure trove of pictures is evidence of the extensive haunted activity at the railroad property.

Just a week earlier, they had already collected a bunch of evidence. According to George, team members reported hearing faint voices and weird noises emanate from the woods around the tracks. When they analyzed the pictures taken during this time, one photo appeared to contain a creepy mist. The team also labeled a perfectly round orb that appeared in the dead center of the path an "angel" spirit.

Often, skeptics insist on seeing some sort of physical evidence. But often investigators process a paranormal encounter on an emotional—and purely subjective—level. In this case, the group could certainly feel the haunting.

"There is so much energy in this area it's hard to believe," George wrote. "The area itself is very active with sounds, soft voices, cracking of wood or branches, feelings of being watched, seeing shadows moving about you, getting a spider web effect on one's body, feelings of headaches, unexplained noises."

What's Behind the Haunting?

The folks in Hamilton Paranormal suggest this little stretch of railroad line is an incredibly haunted spot—and their pictures seem to back up their assumptions that weird forces are at work here. What could be causing a seemingly innocuous piece of railroad real estate to be so paranormally active? Paranormal researchers and railroad historians think it's related to a violent train crash that happened there well over a century ago.

The Hamilton Paranormal team and their friends dug into the local public library archives to find stories from the April 2, 1859 issue of *Harper's Weekly* and the March 21, 1859 issue of the *Times* to offer an explanation for the haunting. According to those accounts, which team members posted on their website, a Great Western Railway freight train had just passed over an embankment near where the haunted activity is centered and encountered no trouble. However, a heavy rain shortly after the train had passed sent plumes of water down the earthen embankment, causing it to give way. The next locomotive to pass—the Express Train East—barreled into what was now a twenty-foot deep chasm. One after another, the engine, the tender, and four more cars fell into the hole. The train carried about sixty passengers that night. Several passengers, the engineer, and a brakeman were listed among the dead. The newspaper reporter indicated that besides the death and injury, the atmosphere that surrounded the accident made the event even more confusing and scary.

The reporter wrote: "The raging of the storm and the darkness of the night added greatly to the intense horrors of the scene and it was some time before the real extent of the calamity was properly understood."

Deaths and intense emotions are often blamed for causing hauntings. Could it be that the deaths, along with the high emotion of this railway accident, are behind the ghostly events near Sydenham Railroad Bridge? It could be. But there might be more to the story and the history of Sydenham Railroad Bridge that is kicking up the supernatural energy.

Other Witnesses

It's not just paranormal researchers who are experiencing weird phenomena at the bridge site.

According to one reader of the *Hamilton Paranormal* blog, named Mike, he had an unexpected brush with the unknown when he and a friend were walking near the scene of the accident in the 1990s. The two were lost in conversation when they heard sounds coming from the top of a nearby cliff. They heard sticks snapping and rocks skipping down the side of the escarpment. The hikers, however, ignored the sounds and kept walking on—until they were forced to pay attention.

Mike said that they continued to cross the bridge's walkway and the sounds continued unabated. Eventually, the sounds seemed to echo from a point directly across from the hikers. Their minds raced to find an explanation—a wild animal? Another hiker?

The hikers moved back toward the path. The sounds kept on their trail.

"There's something there," the friend said.

A debate ensued. Mike said the noises were nothing—just their collective imagination. Mike's friend disagreed. Then, the friend noticed something—and it, whatever *it* was—was either getting bigger, or it was definitely moving toward them.

Witnesses tell us that in these ghostly standoffs, there are two reactions: fight or flight. The writer of the account said he chose the former, at least initially. Mike squatted down and picked up a rock. He boldly announced: "If there's someone over there, I'm throwing a rock!"

The fight strategy didn't last very long. The mysterious figure picked up speed and came so close that the stone limply fell from the witness's hand.

That's when the flight response turned on. The two hikers ran through the trees, thorn bushes ripping at their flesh, and headed toward the safety of a nearby clearing. They turned to see if anything followed them, but whatever was chasing them had stopped the hunt. Their lungs heaving as they tried to catch their breath, the two friends began to compare notes about the strange thing they saw near the railroad tracks to make sure both accounts matched.

"I looked at him and said, 'I don't know what you saw, but this is what I saw…' and I went on to describe it as a large translucent triangle about 2.5–3 feet across with rounded corners," Mike wrote. "It was sort of patchy, it almost looked like a dirty mirror. After my explanation of what I saw, tears started to drip from his eyes, and he said, 'that's exactly what I saw.'"

These would-be paranormal researchers had a few theories of their own. Besides the railroad accident that had occurred just a few yards from where they saw the floating object, they also knew a suicide had occurred near the tracks and that several deadly accidents had happened at a nearby quarry.

Like the investigators of Hamilton Paranormal, Mike's encounter with the railroad spirits of the Sydenham Railroad Bridge was a life-altering experience.

"Anyway that's my story… believe it or not," he concluded. "It has changed my way of thinking."

The Case of the Chatsworth Disaster and the Glowing Grave

Chatsworth, Illinois

If you're in Chatsworth, Illinois, a small town about an hour east of Peoria, and it's a quiet August evening, you might want to stop, stand still, and listen.

Then again, maybe you don't.

Witnesses claim that you can hear the echoes of a train crash from the late 1800s, a train crash so violent that the little town of Chatsworth has never been the same. These witnesses report they've heard the terrible reverberations of twisted locomotive metal and the piercing shrieks of the dying and injured shatter the calmness of a late summer night in an otherwise nondescript Midwestern town.

The story starts on August 11, 1887. It was the early morning and an excursion train was chugging across the dry fields, made exceptionally dry by the scorching heat and lack of rain that summer. Excursion trains operated throughout the country back then, allowing people relatively quick trips to places like Niagara Falls, New York, and Hot Springs, Arkansas. The tourists on this excursion train were just coming back from Niagara Falls, but they had no idea that, for many of the passengers, it would soon turn into an eternal excursion to an unknown destination.

Earlier the previous afternoon, work crews had cleared weeds and brush along the tracks. The men then burned the brush. They were pretty sure they had extinguished the fire before knocking off for the day.

Pretty sure.

A full view of the accident that occurred in Chatsworth, Illinois, on August 11, 1887.

But later that night a wooden bridge near where the men had been working suddenly caught on fire. Some faulted the controlled burn. Some said that was just a coincidence—sparks from a train caused the brush under the bridge to catch fire and eventually spread to the structure itself.

The debate on what had caused the fire, like the fire itself, continues to rage. But there can be no doubt that the fire caused severe damage to the bridge and that the engineer of the excursion train speeding along the long, straight stretch leading out of Chatsworth had no chance to avoid a devastating accident.

According to most accounts, including one that appeared in *Harper's Weekly* in 1887, the train, pulled by two engines, rounded the top of a small hill, giving the engineer a glimpse of the danger ahead. He saw the trestle, now engulfed in flames. But there was no time to stop. Even as he applied the brakes, the first engine passed easily over the bridge, but the engineer said later that he could feel the compromised bridge begin to buckle when the second engine crossed over. The trestle eventually collapsed completely and mayhem soon followed.

The second engine—which was, by the way, officially designated as Engine Number 13—tipped off the tracks. One by one, the following coaches, filled with hundreds of passengers, slammed into the derailed engines and exploded into a mangled heap of metal.

The scene, in a word, was horrifying. But things would get worse. The wreckage caught fire. Passengers caught under parts of the wreckage, or just too injured to move, now found themselves in the midst of a raging brush fire.

Screams and shrieks filled the night air.

Somehow, the first engine stayed on the tracks and two members of the crew commandeered the train and rushed off to get help, blowing the whistle and ringing the bells in alarm. Another crew member ran for help in the opposite direction.

Some survivors, desperately and uselessly, tossed handfuls of dirt onto the blaze.

When the rescuers eventually arrived on the scene, most would carry the horrible memories of the dead and injured with them the rest of their lives. They said the chain reaction seemed to turn the splintering metal into the churning, chaotic blades of some type of monstrous harvester. The bodies were ripped apart and tossed across the land like a thresher discards unusable stalks.

The mixture of terror and tragedy almost guarantees that tales of the supernatural would forever cling to the fields where the accident took so many lives, which, according to various tallies, fluctuated between eighty-one and eighty-five deaths. And those ghost tales still echo. It's not just the scene of the accident that is draped in the anguished cries and shrieks of the past. Some say that the ghosts can also be seen and felt in the buildings of nearby Chatsworth, where bodies were stored awaiting identification and the injured attempted to recover from their wounds. Others say they have watched an odd assortment of lights bobbing through the air near where the excursion train crashed. Experts on the legend suggest these ghostly lights are a supernatural reply to the moment when lantern-wielding rescue workers stumbled onto the horrific accident scene.

Perhaps the weirdest tale is from a graveyard just outside of Chillicothe, Illinois, named LaSalle Cemetery. This story indicates that a survivor of the crash searched through the walls of flames and carnage for his wife. He never found her. In the chaos that followed, somehow the body of his wife was identified as the wife of another man and buried in that man's family plot.

Eventually, authorities straightened out the whole mess and the woman was reburied in LaSalle Cemetery. But a whole other mess was just starting. Over the years, people wandering by or through the cemetery noticed something strange about the woman's tombstone—it glowed at certain times and on certain nights. The grave became a supernatural tourist attraction for teens looking for a late-night thrill and people interested in exploring the supernatural. The eerie glow on the tombstone convinced many that supernatural forces were at work.

Because the accounts were so numerous and because the phenomena appeared so regularly, skeptics also became interested in the site. Their conclusion: headlights, not ghost lights, produced the weird glow on the tombstone. They suggested that if the headlights of cars zooming around the nearby road can catch the stone at just the right angle and at just the right time, the stone looks like it's glowing.

The Screaming Bridge

Avon, Indiana

The bridge that spans White Lick Creek near the town of Avon, Indiana, is an impressive structure to look at. Its concrete spandrel arches and sturdy turn-of-the-twentieth-century construction look particularly picturesque in October when fall foliage is at its height in the Midwest.

That's also the worst time to visit if you're afraid of being exposed to paranormal activity, according to locals. They say that run-ins with the supernatural increase at the Avon Bridge right around Halloween.

What kinds of paranormal activity?

According to people familiar with the bridge haunting, you can hear the ghost of a railroad worker who died during the construction of the bridge. Some say you can hear him moan; others say he screams.

As legend has it, residents of the area considered the construction of the bridge, which is about 70 feet high and 300 feet long, a bit of an engineering marvel for that time period, especially in that area, which, at the time, was largely undeveloped. The project to complete the bridge required considerable expense. And that expense didn't just come in the form of dollars and cents notched down in the ledgers of the Cleveland, Cincinnati, Chicago, and St. Louis Railway, also known as the Big Four Railroad, which built the bridge. The cost also reportedly came in the form of a precious human life.

In one of the more popular renditions of the story, supervisors tasked a group of workers to build support pylons. They framed up the sides and poured the concrete into the center of the structure. Workers considered it a grueling, nerve-rattling, and dangerous task. Standing dozens of feet off the ground and creek, the workers knew that one wrong move, one unfortunate slip, would lead to a deadly fall. The workers, though, in their worse imaginations, could not fathom what happened next. While most of the crew worried more about falling back into the creek bed, one worker fell forward, diving directly into the stony soup of concrete. The mixture quickly enveloped him. For as long as they would live, his colleagues would never quite get over the shriek of the man, nor would they forget his gurgling moans as he finally succumbed to his horrific fate.

The death was reported to the company officials, who made a cold-hearted decision. There would be no attempted rescue effort —he was certainly dead—nor would there be a recovery effort. Building the bridge was costly enough—trying to find the body in the rapidly drying concrete and bringing it back to the surface would cost too much and delay construction too long. The body would remain entombed in the bridge pylon and the bridge would serve as the unfortunate worker's grave.

We mentioned earlier that the sounds of the worker's final shrieks and moans would haunt the surviving workers for the rest of their lives. But that wasn't the only sound that would haunt the men. Later that night, long after quitting time, as the men lingered at the job site, chatting about the day's events in the evening's cool, muted breeze, and as they gathered at fires along the creek bed, the men swore they heard the beating, pounding rhythms of someone slamming their fists against the bridge. There didn't seem to be anyone near the structure, though. Even weirder, the pounding sounded like it was coming from *within* the bridge. Alone with their thoughts of the terrible accident that day, the workers began to wonder if that noise wasn't the sound of the spirit of the dead bridge builder, trying to get out of his concrete tomb.

Ever since then, people have claimed they can hear the same terrifying noises issuing from the bridge—sometimes a rhythmic pounding, not unlike the beats that the bridge builders heard decades ago, but at other times, people say they heard moans waft out of the bridge, and, for the very unlucky, the sounds of shrieks and screams echoing out of the site and reverberating down the creek bed.

Legend also states that the phenomena increase in intensity on the spookiest night of the year: Halloween.

Like a lot of good ghostlore, the tale of Avon's haunted bridge has more than one story attached to it. Another tale identifies a mother who dropped her baby from the bridge as the source of the spectral screams.

Skeptics have an explanation for the phenomena. Since the pylons and other sections of the bridge are hollow, the interior of those supports acts like a huge cement megaphone. When trains go over the bridge, the sounds of their squeaking wheels and clanging cars are amplified. For someone with a good imagination stoked by the creepy vibe of a Halloween evening, the resulting noise could probably sound like a piercing scream of anguish.

Nina Criscuolo, a reporter for WISH TV, a local television station, also did some investigative work. Susan Truax, a local historian, could not find any details of an actual accident at the site that resembled the one referred to in ghost stories told about Avon Bridge. Not everyone agrees with that assessment, though, and even the historian notes that not everything that happened in the early twentieth century made it into the newspapers in that rural community.

One local resident who has family ties that stretch back into the community's history said the only way to test the theory is to go to the Avon Bridge site and listen. "If you go by on Halloween night you'll hear her scream. Yes, you will. The train goes by, you will hear that," Harriett Muston told the reporter.

— Chapter 7 —

HAUNTED RAILROAD PEOPLE

Engineers, Conductors, Brakemen, Workers, and Accident Victims

Ghosts tend to be confined to a building, or a structure. And that tends to be true in railroad ghost stories. You've already read about ghosts who haunt railroad station houses and former station houses, railroad museums, and even bridges and trestles —but railroad ghost stories also have their share of wandering spirits.

Because railroad tracks crisscrossed the country, covering vast and open spaces between cities and towns, some of the railroad ghosts aren't trapped in a building, or on a bridge. They drift along the tracks, often near places where they died in a railroad-related accident, or, more ominously, were murdered.

The wandering railroad spirit has given rise to a unique piece of railroad ghostlore: the ghost light. The pages ahead detail chilling stories—mainly collected from all over the United

States—of headless conductors scouring the tracks for their lost heads, gallant engineers who died in horrific accidents, and disoriented murder victims still wandering the scene of their final breaths. Typically, these spirits appear not as apparitions but as anomalous lights that hover in certain sections of the railroad that mysteriously appear—and, just as inexplicably, vanish.

Skeptics dismiss these sightings as misinterpretation of completely natural phenomena. For instance, headlights reflecting off railroad tracks, depending on the point of view of the observer, may appear to be floating in mid-air.

When possible, arguments from both sides of the paranormal debate will be presented here.

The first story features a pretty impressive figure who had his own encounter with the ghostly lights of a railroad spirit. That person was none other than a president of the United States.

Railroad Ghost Story Gets Presidential Seal of Approval

Maco Station, North Carolina

In 1889, President Grover Cleveland took a swing through North Carolina when he noticed something strange from the window of the presidential train, according to railroad historian James C. Burke. Some of the railroad workers were signaling with two lights, not one, as was typical in those times. He asked an employee of the Atlantic Coast Line why the two-light signal was being used and the answer shocked the leader of the free world.

They told the president that railroad signalmen in the area now carried two lanterns so that the engineers on the train wouldn't mistake them for the infamous Maco Light. There's a good chance that the workers then filled in the president on a variation of a tale that's been told for more than a century about the haunted area of railroad tracks that stretched north to Richmond, Virginia, and south to Florida, east to Birmingham, Alabama, and west to points in North Carolina.

According to one version of the story, right after the Civil War, one of the best brakemen in the business, named Joe Baldwin, stood watch at the last car of a train cruising down the Atlantic Coast Line late at night. Without warning, his car uncoupled from the rest of the train. As the car slowed down, Baldwin knew a train following close behind would crash into the orphan car. He jumped into action, grabbing a lantern, which he then swung with a frantic ferocity. He hoped the engineer of the approaching train would see him and slow his train.

His efforts were in vain.

The train collided with Baldwin's car and, gruesomely, the brakeman—in some versions, he's a conductor—was decapitated.

After that crash, the lonely stretch of rail near Maco Station became known for paranormal activity. Specifically, witnesses claim to see a single light swinging about in the same area where the crash reportedly occurred. People have seen the lights so often and reported them so many times that the site is considered one of the most haunted spots in North Carolina.

Folklore suggests that the lights these people see is Baldwin's lantern, and he is either reenacting his final moments on earth or he is using the light of his lantern to find his head.

John Harden, of Tar Heel Ghosts, told the *Wilmington Star-News* that the light has about the same brightness as a 25-watt bulb, which is about the same level of intensity as a railroad lantern. A few witnesses offer even more detailed descriptions of the Maco Light. They say it's so bright, you could read off of it. Those who have a closer, unobstructed view of the phenomenon also say the light reflects off the rails, causing them to glow.

Over the decades, more than a few paranormal investigation teams—and a bunch of people who are simply intrigued by the possibility of seeing the headless brakeman—have traveled to the area to record their impressions. Those impressions range from deeply skeptical to true believer. Some people say they didn't see the lights at all. Others claim to see the light, swaying back and forth. Still other witnesses say they saw the light, but it didn't sway; the Maco Light remained steady throughout the encounter.

Harden gave the paper the most detailed report of the Maco Light. He said the light appears three feet off the ground, right about where an average-sized brakeman would be holding a lantern. The light always moves east, he added. Most accounts adhere to these specifications, although there are several witnesses who report seeing the light hovering much higher, saying it seemed to sail ten feet off the ground.

"Summer is the popular time for paying the Maco Station Light a visit," Mr. Harden told the newspaper. "Dark and moonless nights are better because they provide a clearer, sharper view."

The light, he added, would appear and disappear like it was on a railroad timetable, usually at fifteen-minute intervals.

Years ago, a Maco Light investigation became the thing to do for the residents of the area, especially the young people of the community.

Brooks Preik was one of the Maco Light enthusiasts. Preik wrote the book *Haunted Wilmington and the Cape Fear Coast.* Preik told the reporter that she grew up near the scene of the Maco Light and heard about it all her life. She added that in the

1960s, she, her husband, and some other couples went to the area.

They waited for about fifteen minutes and didn't see anything. Just as they discussed abandoning the investigation, someone suddenly yelled, "There it is!"

"It was like a full moon on a misty night," she told the *Star-News*. "It appeared in the distance and started coming toward us. It was the eeriest thing I ever saw in my life."

The light seemed to pause about 100 feet away. "We started to run for the car," she continued. "One fellow said, 'I'm not scared of anything,' and started to walk toward the light. The closer he got, the more it would recede."

Preik offers some other tales and possible explanations in her book.

Nearby Fort Bragg soldiers had a more literal approach to ghost hunting. Preik wrote that a machine gun crew went out to bag the light once and for all. According to one version, the crew was out on maneuvers in the area overnight when they spied the light. American soldiers don't like to retreat, so they did what soldiers do best—they attacked. They shot their weapons at the weird light but came no closer than any other witness in figuring out the light's source. After they shot a few rounds with marksman-like accuracy, the light continued to bounce around, seemingly impervious to the bullets.

Natural Explanations?

So, how much of the Joe Baldwin legend is true? Or is it just ghostlore?

We'll start with the tale of Joe Baldwin. According to local historians, most of the story seems to be made-up. Although a

Charles Baldwin was listed as a victim of a railroad accident that happened years before the mishap that reportedly claimed Joe Baldwin's life, there are no railroad records or newspaper articles that suggest a railroad worker—or anyone—named Joe Baldwin died in an accident at that time, or at the site where the light has been seen. There doesn't seem to be any record of a decapitation on the lines, either. A decapitation is a gruesome accident and would have likely made the paper. A few railroad-related accidents did occur, of course, including one where the railroad worker died a few days later. But he didn't die on the tracks as the Maco Light story suggests.

Debunking the Maco Light became so popular that a lot of scientists and paranormal researchers investigated the sighting and produced their own theories. Their explanations range across the scientific spectrum.

The Smithsonian Institute and world-famous parapsychologist J. B. Rhine investigated the phenomena, for example. Rhine thought headlights from automobiles might be behind the lights. But others point out that witnesses have been reporting the lights since long before the advent of automobiles.

And, of course, several officials offered the skeptical explanation-du-jour on the Maco Light, as they do with most UFO or ghost stories that challenge rational and natural explanations: swamp gas.

Still, the reports, and even some evidence, began to flow in and captured national attention. *Life* published a spread on the lights but didn't capture a photograph of the phenomena. Photographers for the *Star-News*, who paid regular visits to the area, had a little more luck. They often captured pictures of the eerie lights—or, at least some type of eerie lighting effects—in the area.

However, most skeptics consider the best of these photographic representations of the Maco Light to be unconvincing. It also doesn't help that the photographs, taken before the digital photography era, are now available on grainy microfilm.

Disappearing Lights

By the 1970s, the Maco Light, which appeared and disappeared so regularly, had finally faded out forever, according to most of the residents in the area and experts on the case. There are a few explanations for the lack of recent sightings. Use of that rail line dropped, and eventually crews tore up the tracks. Booming growth brought in more people who built homes and businesses nearby.

There's a more hopeful explanation. Some hope that ole Joe Baldwin finally found his head and lived happily—and re-capitated—ever after: finally, a well-deserved eternal retirement.

The Paulding Light

Paulding, Michigan

Located in Michigan's Upper Peninsula, Paulding is a small community in Ontonagon County. But what it lacks in size and population, it more than makes up for in mysterious phenomena and intense debates on the explanation of that mysterious phenomena.

The Paulding Light accounts are told throughout the region and have received nationwide attention recently. The history of the Paulding Light stretches back decades at the very least and may or may not be related to the region's considerable railroad legacy. Since the 1960s, witnesses have seen light orbs dancing in a valley just outside of Paulding. There are a lot of natural explanations, including swamp gas and headlights from cars traveling down a nearby road, but citizens tend to favor a tale that involves, like a few other stories, a heroic railroad brakeman.

According to this legend, a railroad line was once built at the very site where the lights appear. One night, a train had stalled on the tracks. Before the use of radio communications, if a train stalled on the tracks, workers had to hop a ride on the shoe-leather express to find a telephone or a railroad station to let the main office know about the situation. Of course, this could be risky, as well. A train stalled around a blind curve, or at the bottom of a steep decline, could find itself a sitting duck for a violent collision.

According to a tale that's part of the Paulding Light legend (also referred to as the Dog Meadow Light), that's exactly what happened to a locomotive that stalled one night at a vulnerable spot near Paulding. In this story, a brakeman saw an oncoming train and hurried from the stranded train, swinging his lantern. The approaching engine drew closer and closer but made no attempt to stop. The brakeman figured that the engineer wasn't looking at the side of the tracks and failed to see his lantern. He made the bold decision to jump in front of the train to get the engineer's attention. It worked, but with horrifying results. The engineer did slow the train down and was able to signal for a hard brake to avoid complete catastrophe, the legend goes, but the brakeman could not jump out of the way in time and died in his valiant attempt to stop the train. The mysterious light that floats about three feet off the ground is the ghost of the heroic brakeman, still swinging his lamp and trying to attract the attention of the engineer, according to numerous tales about the Paulding Light.

Residents have other railroad-related reasons for the anomalous lighting. They say that an engineer was murdered near where the lights engage in their eerie dance.

Skeptics Respond

As noted in other tales of railroad paranormal in this book, accounts of the dancing lights of a dead railroad worker attract three types of people: believers in the supernatural who are looking to confirm their beliefs, the curious who want to find evidence for the unexplained, and skeptics who are out to find natural explanations for the phenomena. That latter group has long since seized on a mission to take the super out of the supernormal activity of the Paulding Light.

Since the 1960s, several scientific groups and skeptical organizations have made the trek to Paulding to examine the evidence. One of those groups to investigate the Paulding Light included a team of science students from nearby Michigan Tech. They released their conclusion with the *Michigan Tech News*, the university news source. The students say it's nothing more than headlights from a nearby road. One team member went to a spot where he could log each time a car drove along the road. The rest of the team logged each time the lights appeared. Sure enough, the arrival of the cars correlated with sightings of the lights.

The other clue is that reports of the lights started to circulate in the 1960s, about the time when cars began to routinely travel through the area.

But, hold on, Paulding Light believers counter: there were reports of lights prior to the 1960s, including a few at the turn of the century. And some reports suggest the lights are seen far from the highway. Finally, believers say that a team of investigators from *Fact or Faked: Paranormal Files*, a show that tries to prove or debunk evidence of paranormal phenomena, could not find natural explanations for the Paulding Light case. It could be that while car headlights explain some of the sightings, maybe there are others that defy the explanation.

Now, whether or not these other explanations for the lights include the lantern clutched in the hand of the spirit of a departed heroic brakeman is a completely different story.

A Spectral Brakeman Who Never Takes a Break

Brockway, Pennsylvania

The Pennsylvania town is now called Brockway, but its original name was Brockwayville, before being shortened in the 1920s. The town once prospered as an important railroad town nestled along the Little Toby Creek.

Curving their way into the heart of Pennsylvania's coal and timber region, trains pushed through the mountainous region day and night, carrying supplies into the coal mines and factories and hauling away tons and tons of the precious black rocks and timber. Shepherding the beastly long and heavily loaded trains up and down the mountains and around the twists and turns of the line took a special locomotive crew. Just like the well-oiled engines the railroad crew piloted, the workers had to be in sync, knowing exactly what the other members of the crew were doing, even though they may have been separated by several cars.

Howard Neusbaum, a young brakeman, was on one of those special crews. He had established a reputation as being one of the best brakemen in the business after just a few short years. Neusbaum was assigned to serve as a brakeman on a return trip of empty cars from Clermont, a town north of Brockway. The engineer carefully piloted the unwieldy snake of cars through a particularly treacherous part of the journey.

Operating trains in rolling terrains—where one steep drop is immediately met with a slow uphill climb—can be tricky. The opposing forces of gravity weighing the train down, and the engine's power trying to move it forward, can build pressure that uncouples the cars. It's almost like a twig snapping.

A newspaper article describes it like this: "A sharp grade pitches into a 'hole' out of which another steep grade breaks abruptly." The stretch of track where Neusbaum was operating had a few sections where a train could "break." The newspaper account continues to say that most of the time, a break could be fixed; other times, the uncoupled cars could take off on their own, turning the well-controlled rolling stock into a deadly runaway train.

That's what happened to Neusbaum's crew. The train uncoupled and the crew never had a chance to check it. One section of train collided with the other and eighteen cars, including several occupied by the crew members, were thrown from the tracks.

Once the shock of the accident wore off, the crew members who were tossed from the train collected themselves and began to look for survivors. They called names and waited for replies. They called Howard's name. There was no reply. They just heard the icy silence of night and felt their hearts drop into the pits of their stomachs.

Like many railroad tales, there are a few versions of this story. Ed Kelemen, in his book *Pennsylvania's Haunted Railroads*, reports that Neusbaum died in an accident at a switching yard in

Kane, Pennsylvania. And switching yards were particularly dangerous places for brakemen at that time.

What all versions seem to agree on is that everyone liked the brakeman—and Neusbaum's death would remain in the minds of his coworkers when he began to show up—seemingly—in the flesh. Crews, particularly brakemen, began to see the ghost of Neusbaum. In many cases, he would appear just as a train began to navigate its way through a tricky section of tracks near Brockwayville.

Railroad ghosts aren't always identified, but because many of the railroaders knew Neusbaum before he died, they recognized him immediately when he appeared. Reports suggest that he continues to show up to railroaders working in the area.

While most ghosts inspire fear in witnesses, that's not the case with Neusbaum's ghost. Many workers who have experienced the haunting said that after the initial surprise of seeing the apparition wore off, they reportedly felt relieved that this unexpected—but not unwelcome—passenger had hopped a ride on their train. In fact, they considered him a helpful ghost, who assisted the crew as they made their way along their often-perilous journey.

In a way, the brakeman has become a sort of patron saint of engineers and their crew.

1888 Ghost Rider of the Rails

Cheyenne, Wyoming

The freight train pulled out from Cheyenne, Wyoming, right on time, according to W.H. Smith, a well-respected conductor of the Denver Pacific Railroad. About fifteen miles outside of Cheyenne, though, there's a notorious hill on the line, called Big Springs. This stretch of railway called for the crew to precisely handle the long beast of a train—and, especially, the crew's brakemen would need to be at the top of their game. They knew if the train picked up too much speed, it could lose control, fly off the tracks around one of the turns, and cascade down the mountainside.

The men on the freight train also knew a few factors were outside of the crew's control, according to Jerome Clark, author of *Unnatural Phenomena: A Guide to the Bizarre Wonders of North America*. In 1884, four years before Smith's own crew was attempting to navigate the precarious section of track, a freight train hit a broken track and derailed, Clark reported. One person —a brakeman—died in the accident.

Smith thought his train was picking up too much speed and gave the engineer the signal to blow the whistle and start to apply the brakes. As the whistle wailed, Smith watched his brakemen jump into action and twist the brake wheels to slow the big freight down. Well, not all of them. Both the rear brakeman and the one further up the train were on the job, but another brakeman, the one responsible for the middle section of the train, just sat on the brake wheel. Smith nudged his rear brakeman to call attention to the slacker and they both watched as the man refused to budge. They decided to confront him. As they came close to the man, though, he stood up and nonchalantly stepped right off the train. Smith and his colleague, both horrified, rushed to the scene and peered out onto the ground below, expecting to see the battered remains of the suicidal brakemen. But, to their shock, they saw no one. He had just disappeared.

The crew later found out that the phantom brakeman had appeared to other railroad crews working the area. Just a week before Smith reported his encounter, a brakeman on another train said that he was setting the brakes on the train when he turned to find a brakeman sitting on the brake wheel about three cars back, exactly like the figure in Smith's encounter. The brakeman went about his business, moving up another three cars before looking back at the strange figure. Then, the worker became concerned. This stranger had followed him and was now sitting on the wheel of the brake that the brakeman had set only a few moments before.

The brakeman shouted to his foreman and they both stood and watched as the man stood up and, just as Smith had reported in his account, stepped off the train.

Stories of phantom brakemen and helper spirits pop up throughout railroad ghostlore, but the story of the Cheyenne specter is different in both the number of sightings as well as the quality of witnesses who claimed to see the strange, ghostly sighting. The workers had impeccable reputations among their colleagues.

In an 1888 *Indiana Democrat* account of the incidents cited by Clark, the newspaper reporter wrote, "Neither of the railroad men who tell this peculiar story is a bit suspicious and both were in their soberest senses when this peculiar apparition appeared to them."

A Not-So-Thankful Thanksgiving Day Haunting

Geneva, New York

On Thanksgiving Day in 1902, a train chugged along the tracks right outside of Geneva, New York. As it started to cross the Marsh Bridge, the engineer and fireman heard a terrifying shriek. When they looked up, a white figure stood on the tracks, wildly flailing his arms to get their attention. That definitely worked.

The train crew slammed on the brakes—as much as a train's brakes can be slammed—and managed to bring the beast to a standstill.

Another scream pierced the forest surrounding the train.

They watched as the freaky figure disappeared.

Not sure about what they had on their hands—nothing in the train operator's manual covered what to do when encountering shrieking forest weirdos on the tracks—the workers clambered off the engine and began to inspect the track while looking into the forest for any sign of whomever had hailed, or screamed at the train to stop. Nothing was amiss with the track. And there was no sign of the shrieking apparition.

They started to cross the bridge and one final shriek rattled across the bridge.

The train chugged down the line and into the station where the men knew they had one whopper of a haunted railroad story to tell their colleagues. After they finished their story of encountering the shrieking freak, the railroad workers received a knowing nod from their captivated audience. From the description of where the encounter took place, the listeners said they likely encountered a ghost from a serious train accident. The townsfolk said that only a few Thanksgivings before this run-in with the shrieking ghost, a train had derailed on the Marsh Bridge, killing the engineer and fireman.

Rescuers who went to the scene could only recover the body of the engineer. The body of the fireman either drifted downstream or got bogged down in the quicksand-like soil under the bridge.

Since then, the shrieking ghost returns every Thanksgiving. The speculation is that it's the ghost of the fireman—who never had a proper burial—returning to the scene of the fateful accident.

Truth or Folklore?

A train wreck. A haunted fireman. A haunted anniversary. They are all necessary ingredients of railroad ghostlore tales. But is there any truth to the bizarre legend?

Luckily, Jennifer Jones, of *The Dead History*, who was mentioned in the chapter about Ogden Railroad hauntings, has done some outstanding paranormal detective work on this one too. Her conclusion? Maybe.

Based on her findings, an actual incident fits most of the shrieking ghost narrative. On March 29, 1875, a train pulled out of Syracuse and headed toward Rochester. Right outside of Geneva—exactly where the ghost accosted the Thanksgiving train—flood waters had rushed over the Marsh Creek Bridge. The water was just high enough to cause the engine, the tender, and baggage car to leave the track and topple into the raging river. Just as the details of the ghost story point out, the engineer, Ignatius Buelte, and fireman, Augustus Sipple, were swept off the engine and into the flood waters. Both bodies were later discovered downstream.

Two key points differ: searchers did recover the body of the fireman, and the incident did not happen on Thanksgiving.

Jones believes this may be another example of how history, ghost stories, and folklore mix together.

"Maybe this is one of those urban legends meant to remind people how fleeting life can be," she wrote in her blog. "Or maybe engineer Buelte and fireman Sipple were simply trying to warn other railroad men of the dangers of the bridge."

He May Have Died at His Station but He Left a Restless Spirit

Atchison, Kansas

The early days of railroading are full of stories of unbelievable heroism—and tales of unforgivable cowardice. Railroad history would place engineer Brit (sometimes referred to as Bert) Craft in the former category.

In the summer of 1882, Craft sat in the cab of his engine, carefully shepherding his mail train out of Cawker City, Kansas. People considered Craft to be the best engineer in the business. When the railroad's big bosses wanted to travel by rail, they asked Craft to serve as an engineer.

Nobody knows when Craft got the first inkling of danger ahead. Some speculate that maybe a puff of smoke wafting from just around a sharp bend signaled him. But it's likely Craft only had seconds to respond when he guided the engine around the bend and saw that the small bridge, which crosses the dry creek bed near Great Spirit Spring, was completely engulfed in flames. The fire damaged the integrity of the structure and, as soon as the heavy train tested the beams, they cracked. The engine—along with the mail and express cars—fell into the creek bed. The passenger cars, though, remained on the burning bridge. Somehow, members of the crew survived the crash and, once they extricated themselves from the wreckage, ran to rescue the passengers in the blaze.

Thanks to the heroic work of Craft and his crew, many passengers escaped the conflagration. Craft wasn't so fortunate, though. During the rescue effort, steam escaping from the damaged engine badly scalded Craft, the fireman, and the conductor, according to an account. The fireman died immediately, but Craft died later as a result of the injuries.

Craft's family buried the hero in a nearby cemetery. His gravestone is etched with a simple saying: "He died at his station."

His heroic spirit, though, lives on, based on several encounters reported by witnesses.

For more than a century, strange accounts have filled the railroad lines near the Atchison area, accounts that many paranormal theorists say are related to Craft's heroic actions during that hot summer day in 1882.

Just a few weeks after the accident, a newspaper reporter from the *Kansas Globe* took a break on the porch of a store in West Atchison. He struck up a conversation with a group of Central Branch railroad workers, including a freight engineer and his fireman. The engineer began to tell the reporter a bizarre story. He said he had engineered a train a few nights before that was approaching the bridge where Craft and members of his crew perished. As he drew closer, an engine whistle ripped through the night. *There should definitely not be traffic on the line at this time*, thought the shocked engineer, He leaned his head out of the cab window to see what was going on and saw a crazy sight. Within a hundred yards of the bridge, an eerie outline of an engine came around the curve, directly at the engineer.

Too shocked to take evasive action, the engineer froze, expecting the worst. But even more mysteriously, the phantom train abruptly vanished.

The reporter noted the earnestness of the engineer when he told his story—and particularly when he revealed one detail. The engineer told the reporter that the ghost train looked like someone had outlined the train with hand-drawn white lines, and that he had noticed that leaning out of the window of that phantom engine was, without a doubt, Brit Craft. He was stoically staring down the line.

The engineer apologized for how ridiculous the story sounded, but the fireman on that train offered some verification. He said that he happened to look up while working and saw that the engineer was "white as death." As they passed the bridge, the engineer told him, "I have seen the ghost of Brit Craft's engine."

Reports of the haunted engine began to barrage railroad company authorities and newspaper reporters. Train crews reported seeing the white-outlined engine right before the break of day in three different places between the towns of Downs and Beloit.

Craft, apparently, isn't tethered to his phantom train. Other people have seen a light glowing alongside the tracks near where the train crashed. They think it's the ghost of the area's most famous engineer who now wanders the lonely railroad tracks at night, joining dozens of other specters who supposedly inhabit Atchison, Kansas, one of the America's most haunted towns.

There's another legend attached to Craft and his haunted engine. According to this tale, the engine might also be cursed. After the deadly accident, crews repaired the engine that Craft had operated during the accident. Just a little over a year after the first accident, Craft's engine—Central Branch engine number 162—smashed into an obstruction just about a mile away from the first accident. The engine was badly damaged, possibly beyond repair, according to the newspaper account.

Maybe Craft decided if he couldn't pilot ol' 162, nobody should.

The Natural State Boasts Some Supernatural Railroad Tales

Gurdon and Cossette, Arkansas

When it comes to anomalous activity, Arkansas, also known as the Natural State, is anything but natural. You might say it's the Supernatural State.

Arkansas is full of legends about ghosts and tales of the paranormal, according to occult theorists. The supernaturally charged environment of Arkansas also powers a flurry of haunted railroad stories. While ghost chasers across the country report that mysterious lights appear along railroad tracks and crossings in their home states, Arkansas has two major railroad spook light manifestations. The first that we'll discuss—the Gurdon Light—occurs in Clark County, Arkansas, and the second appears near Crossett, Arkansas.

Money, Murder, and Mysterious Lights

Times were tough during the Great Depression—and time is money. And that's what started the disastrous chain of events that apparently still haunts the tracks near the town of Gurdon, about eighty-five miles south of Little Rock, Arkansas.

According to the legend, in 1931, a railroad worker named Louis McBride felt the company he worked for—the Missouri-Pacific Railroad—had cheated him out of how many days he would be allowed to work. In the Depression, cutting hours meant cutting pay and, to some workers, that seemed like the company was stealing food from the worker's table and right out of their family's mouths. McBride decided to address the situation with his supervisor, William McClain.

Let's just say the conversation didn't go so well.

As the argument grew increasingly more volatile, McBride picked up a shovel and beat McClain over the head with it. Then he took a hammer that was used to drive railroad spikes into the ground and began to bludgeon McClain with the instrument. McClain's murder caused a sensation in the relatively peaceful area. But as the buzz about the murder swept through Gurdon, another spectacle began to seize the attention of the residents. People started to see a strange light dancing along the railroad tracks near the site of the infamous crime.

The light, which floated in midair, had the same shape and intensity of a railroad lantern. It didn't take long for the witnesses to suggest that the source of this light was none other than William McClain's lantern—or, at least, the lantern of William McClain's ghost.

As with other cases of will-o'-wisps that appear near railroad tracks and facilities, believers and debunkers clashed over the Gurdon lights. Believers even debated among themselves. Some say that the lights are caused by McClain's lanterns, while others believe that a decapitated railroad worker is using a phantom lantern to look for his head, which is a common theme that appears in railroad ghostlore.

Skeptics don't buy that the lights are either the ghost of a murder or an accident victim. They say the phenomena are caused by car headlights from a nearby highway. However, the strange lights seem to pre-date the existence of the road in question. They also suggest the lights are just a random manifestation of an electrical effect, called the piezoelectric effect.

So, the debate, just like an old phantom railroad lantern—whether it's clutched by either old man McClain, or the ghost of some poor headless conductor—seems doomed to continue for an eternity in this sleepy section of Arkansas.

The Beheaded Brakeman of Crossett

Located in the southeast corner of Arkansas, the town of Crossett grew up around the papermaking industry. To fuel the processes used to make paper, factory owners needed a railroad. Eventually, the fate of the town, the paper mills, and the people became entwined with the trains that brought in the raw material and transported the finished product to market.

The fates of some railroad workers, however, were tied much tighter to those rails—and sometimes those fates turned to misfortune.

That would certainly be the case for a brakeman who worked on a train traveling just outside of Crossett. According to the legend, the worker fell on the track and was decapitated. Since then, people have reported seeing a weird light dancing along the tracks. One thing that's really strange about these orbs is that when witnesses start to move toward the lights to investigate further, they immediately disappear.

Obviously, most people connect the phenomena with that brakeman. Others say the light has an even more heartbreaking origin. These folks believe that it's not a headless railroad worker haunting Crossett's railroad tracks but his wife, who is carrying a lantern in a vain attempt to find the remains of her husband.

From all accounts, she's still looking.

Northern Spook Light: Canada's Famous Railway Ghost Light

St. Louis, Saskatchewan

St. Louis, Saskatchewan, is a small, agricultural village that rests on the South Saskatchewan River in Canada. Most people know it as a picturesque and peaceful community. But it has a much bigger reputation among fans of railroad history and believers in paranormal phenomena. St. Louis is the epicenter for the eponymous St. Louis lights, a ghastly light show that appears without warning and seems to be connected to the village's railroad past.

For more than a century, people have claimed to see lights—a bright white light that looks like the light on a train engine and a red light that resembles a railroad lantern—appear along the train tracks, located just outside of the village. Some say they have heard animal noises—coyotes and wolves howling and geese honking—right before the appearance of the lights. The phenomenon happens so often and so regularly that just about everyone in town has a story to tell—and people actually travel to the village in hopes of seeing the lights.

One witness, Edward Lussier, of St. Louis, told a reporter from the *Western Producer* that he saw the lights.

"When I was growing up in my teens... we used to go there quite a bit on weekends and if you sat on the track and looked south down the train track, the light would appear periodically," said Lussier.

One night, Lussier and several relatives went to see the lights. Lussier and his cousin followed his father and uncle as they walked along the tracks. His mother and aunt stayed in the car. As they walked, a bright light suddenly flashed behind them and cast their silhouettes on the tracks so plainly that Lussier's father and uncle turned around and saw the lights.

"Dad came running 'cause he thought we'd be scared and we hadn't even noticed, we didn't see the light ourselves, so that was kind of an eerie thing," Lussier told the reporter.

St. Louis's own mayor, Les Rancout, is one of the witnesses, according to the *Western Reporter*.

"It basically looks like a street light from a distance that's a little brighter and gets a little dimmer and there's a little red light that's sometimes seen on either side of it," said Rancourt.

The mayor's attention to detail reveals the heart of the controversy about the ghost train lights. Some say the bright white lights and the trailing red lights point to a natural explanation for the phenomena. In fact, two teens won a science prize by theorizing that the lights are headlights and taillights from cars, according to the *Western Reporter*. The teens asked one of their fathers to drive to a spot south of the tracks. When he flashed his headlights, the girls saw the ghost train lights. When he flashed his taillights, the girls could see the little red light that is often described in St. Louis Light encounters.

Phenomenon Debunked?

Not everyone thinks the young scientists' explanation matches their own experience. Some have tried to replicate the experiment at places where they saw the lights and failed to see the headlights and taillights when their confederates flashed them. Maybe the headlights can explain some of the sightings, but not all, these debunker-debunkers counter. A NASA scientist couldn't explain the phenomenon and a television crew shut down the highway and still saw the lights. Others say that the lights predate the construction of the highway and perhaps even the invention of the car. That would rule out headlights for that era. Reports do coincide with the arrival of rail service to the area, however.

While believers try to debunk the skeptics' debunking, they put forth their own explanation, and it relates to Canada's railroad past. In fact, there are a bunch of explanations. According to one legend, a train was rolling north on the tracks that lead to St. Louis when the conductor jumped off the caboose to inspect the track. The worker, however, slipped and fell under the train. The wheels decapitated him. Some people believe that the light is the headlamp of the ghost train's engine and the little red lights are a grim reenactment of the conductor scanning the track with a lantern to find his severed head.

There's another gruesome tale to explain the visitation of the St. Louis ghost train. According to this version, which occurs possibly in the 1930s, a heavy snow blocked the tracks, causing a train carrying mail to halt just outside of St. Louis. The stranded train presented too tempting of a target to a pair of thieves. They rushed down on the train, but a brave conductor confronted the thieves and a fight broke out. Outnumbered, the conductor gave a good account of himself, but the thieves eventually got the upper hand and killed the railroad worker. Flush with booty from the train, it didn't take long for the honor among thieves to crumble. One of the thieves killed the other to seize all the loot. The lights that people now see is a paranormal replay of that fateful attack on the mail train and the conductor's valiant defense of railroad people and property.

The debates continue about the St. Louis Ghost Train: Is it a real paranormal phenomenon, or just a mistaken natural phenomenon? One thing is for certain, there's no other haunted railroad phenomenon that is so famous and so consistent that a national government officially recognized it. In 2014, the Canada post administration issued a stamp commemorating the St. Louis Ghost Train lights, joining other creepy Canadian tales, including the Maritimes' Northumberland Strait ghost ship, Quebec's ghost of the Count of Frontenac, Ontario's Fort George Spirits of 1812, and Alberta's Ghost Bride.

Oh, and the day that the St. Louis Ghost Train stamp was issued? June 13, which, of course, was a Friday.

The Suitor House: Canada's Spirit Weigh Station

Calgary, Alberta

On paper, the Suitor House, an historic property in Calgary, Alberta, has all the right qualifications for the ultra-haunted house. At one time, the home served as a hospital where officials isolated patients from Calgary's healthy population. But it wasn't a hospital in the sense that doctors hoped the patients would get better. It was basically a place where they could die.

You might think that would be the reason behind the ghostly goings-on in the house, but according to experts on Calgary's haunted history, the spirit that continues to inhabit the Suitor House isn't the ghost of a patient, or even a doctor. The home is haunted by the ghost of a widow whose husband died in a bizarre railroad mishap. According to the tale, a young couple lived in a third-floor apartment in the building. The husband used the freight trains that would snake through Calgary as a way to get around the city. He would jump on one train near the home, take it as far as he could to get close to his eventual destination, and then jump off.

He did it so often that it became routine. But, then, just when his confidence was up and his guard was down, he tried to jump onto the train but missed. His legs were crushed under the wheels of the train. Horrifically, some accounts say that he tried to crawl to a nearby hospital, but he never made it.

Here's where a twist occurs in the story. You might think it's the husband who haunts the Suitor House. However, paranormal theorists now blame the haunted activity not on the husband, but on the man's wife. She still stays in the home, waiting for her husband to return.

On a few occasions, people who have stayed at a nearby bed and breakfast raised complaints with the owner of the Suitor House. They told the owner that a female Suitor House resident is really unfriendly. They tried to wave at her when she stood on the balcony and they even tried to talk to her, but she completely dismissed them, like they weren't even there. The owner asked for a description of the mean lady. The witnesses described her as young with dark, curly hair.

No one at the Suitor House, however, matched that description.

Still other people say they see a woman looking out of the window and down onto the bike path that used to be the railroad tracks where the accident occurred. Some have even snapped pictures of the forlorn lady.

Inside the home, workers claim to hear the sounds of things moving around—or someone moving stuff around—on the third floor. When they go to investigate, the floor is vacant.

While there are a lot of homes rumored to be haunted and properties that have inspired railroad ghostlore, believers say the Suitor House is different because visitors have collected photographic evidence. On more than one occasion, a person will snap a picture of the beautiful old home, hoping to memorialize the visit, but when they inspect their photos, they notice something different, something strange that wasn't in the home when they took the picture. In one of the third-floor windows of the Suitor House, these accidental spirit photographers and would-be paranormal investigators notice a woman looking at them from the window. She doesn't look anything like any of the other visitors, or any of the current occupants.

But she does fit the description of the woman who lost her young husband in a tragic railroad accident many years ago.

Dead Worker's Ghost Gives Whole New Meaning to Being "Fired"

Eddystone, Pennsylvania

During its long history as a leading steam locomotive manufacturer, the Baldwin Locomotive Works produced more than 70,000 train engines, most of them steam-powered. The company, initially located in Philadelphia, and later Eddystone, Pennsylvania, built sprawling manufacturing sites that arguably produced more engines than any other American company; they made thousands of engines that powered the Allied victories in World War I and World War II.

Of course, large manufacturing sites are susceptible to accidents, some of them horrific in cost and scope. Baldwin was no exception. Its history is marked by a few major accidents. Some of the deadliest of these mishaps, it seems, refuse to be a mere tally in the loss column of the company ledger, or a distant memory stored in the archives of the town newspaper. In one case, the ghost of a worker continued to punch in days long after an accident took his life.

A punching machine in the boiler shop of the Baldwin Locomotive Works in Philadelphia, Pennsylvania.

On August 26, 1902, the *Wilkes-Barre News* reported that James McGlone, a laborer in the Baldwin Locomotive Works, claimed to see the ghost of a worker who had died in the plant just a few days before.

He told the paper that his foreman barked out a command to find a large monkey wrench. He remembered seeing it behind a bunch of boilers. The huge boilers sat in front of the furnaces that belched out flames, which licked out of the iron bars like vipers' tongues toward McGlone. Even though the roar of the furnaces drowned out nearly every noise on the floor, the foreman and his men could hear the cry of McGlone.

Thinking McGlone had fallen or he had been caught up in some other type of accident, the men rushed to his aid. A recent accident that had claimed the lives of a few workers, no doubt, weighed heavily on their minds and caused them to drop everything and bolt toward McGlone's aid.

He was not hurt, thankfully, but he seemed distraught. When he finally managed to form words in his mouth, McGlone shouted, "Oh Tom! Tom!"

McGlone, considered one of the crew's strongest and most reliable workers, had fainted. His coworkers immediately called for help and had him transported to a nearby hospital. McGlone remained unconscious for about a half hour before he awoke. But he was still distraught.

When he came to and calmed a little, he told the medical team a fantastic story. He said he was scouring the area for the tool when he felt a strange sensation. He had never felt something like this in his life and found it difficult to put the sensation into words. When pressed, though, he said it felt like someone was there—even though he knew he was alone—and that someone was watching him.

When he turned to the furnace, there, in the glare of the flames that lapped out of the furnace door, McGlone saw Tom, the man who had died in a recent accident.

"He just stood there and looked at me with an awful, sad, faraway look in his eyes," the stricken man told his doctors. The vision—or ghost, or whatever it was—terrified McGlone so much that he fell to the floor and buried his face in his hands.

"I feel ten years older today than I did yesterday," he added.

The paper was quick to clear McGlone of any character issues that might have caused the vision. The doctors said he wasn't drinking at the time of the incident, nor did he seem susceptible to hallucinations.

The doctors admitted they were reluctant to believe McGlone's story, but the medical effects of the vision were real. They kept him in the hospital, treating him for shock, until they finally released him and let him go back home.

No one else reported any other ghostly incidents in the manufacturing facility.

—— Conclusion ——

TRAVELOGUE FOR A TRIP ON THE HAUNTED RAILS

So, we've come to the final stop on our long ride into the heart of haunted railroads. And what a ride it's been. There have been stories that suggest that people have seen ghosts of railroad people, places, and things. Railroad museums count more than a few ghosts in their exhibits. Spirits of engineers, conductors, workers, and firemen still lurk near the tracks where they died, say some paranormal theorists. Railroad facilities—factories, station houses, and even bridges and tunnels—teem with specters and spooks.

Haunted rails are not unique to the United States—in fact, it's a global phenomenon. Railroad ghost stories are told in Canada, England, Sweden, and other spots around the world.

These paranormal tales on rails just don't seem to be a relic of the long past, a time, cynics sneer, when people were much more superstitious. These ghost stories pop up during all time periods, from the long past to the modern era. And new stories of the railroad supernatural are coming to the surface all the time.

So, what are we to make of these strange tales of headless conductors, haunted cabooses, and hellish curses that seem etched deeply into the fabric of railroad history and folklore? And why are there so many of these types of stories?

I've wondered about these questions, too, as I've researched and written this book. In fact, one of the reasons that I started compiling these stories is because of a folktale that I heard when I was a kid. This story began with a railroad worker—conductor or brakeman or just an employee of the Pennsylvania Railroad, depending on who tells the story—who was on his way home. In some stories, he is too tired to make it home; in others, he's just, well, too drunk. He falls asleep on the path next to the train tracks, but somehow he either sleepwalks or passes out, right on the tracks. A train rolls by and our sleepy—or inebriated—railroad worker is decapitated.

Now, the legend warns, if you're out late at night, wandering along the tracks, you just might meet up with the headless railroad worker who is still searching for his head. Who needs the railroad police keeping watch over company property when you have a headless phantom around the yard?

I've never talked to anyone who had a verified run-in with the ghost of this unfortunate railroad worker and, as I've found while researching this book, stories of mangled railroad workers are classic bits of railroad ghostlore. In this volume, of course, we've encountered similar themes in railroad stories around the country and throughout the world.

These railroad ghost stories remind me more of the university ghost stories that I wrote about in *America's Haunted Universities* and *Haunted World War II* and, perhaps to a lesser extent, in my books about haunted rock and roll and country music. In the latter volumes, I felt there was a connection between the consciousness-raising potential of music and the supernatural, or, at least, tales of the supernatural.

Railroad ghost stories drive right to history's core. They don't just tell us about spooks and spirits; they tell us about the power of the railroad, a technology that rewrote history. And these stories tell us about brave men and women confronted with a technology that could be just as dangerous and destructive as it was vital and productive.

Historians may chafe at my suggestion that ghost stories make good history—and I would agree with that criticism. However, I'll use a railroad analogy to explain why this criticism might be slightly off the rails. If history serves as the main line of railroad ghost stories, tales of the strange and supernatural railroad incidents, like other ghostly tales, can serve as feeder lines to real historical accounts. People read a story about a wandering railroad engineer spirit, for example, which then sparks their interest to confirm the tale, or it just whets the intellectual curiosity enough to cause the reader or listener to learn more about local railroad history.

As proof, remember the story about the Malvern Murder. A ghost story that two men heard when they were kids prompted them to become amateur anthropologists, uncovering evidence of a terrible epidemic—or a terrible murder.

There's another related reason for the popularity of railroad ghost stories: they can serve as cautionary tales. I joked about the ghost of the headless railroad worker serving as an eternally vigilant security guard along the rails of his former employer. But, might there be some truth to this? I speculate that some of these ghost stories may have had a similar origin. Would it be so outlandish to suspect that smart railroad company executives seeking to protect millions of dollars' worth of equipment and freight might decide to post a spooky headless ghost on their property—or, at least to not discourage the passing of a haunted rumor?

Ghost stories of accident victims or maimed workers at certain sites may also be passed from worker to worker to raise awareness of dangerous spots along the line that require special care and attention from the crew.

Finally, shared points on the philosophical and technological timeline may reveal another theory about why railroad history is so haunted. As the railroad industry spread exponentially across the country, spiritualism—a belief system that focuses on the communion of spirits and ghosts—exploded across the country at about the same time. Ghost stories and tales of railroad heroics and tragedy may have mixed to create this unique type of ghostlore.

Now, let's make sure to address the 800-pound ghost gorilla in the room.

Not all of the stories in this book are ghostlore, technically speaking. For a story to be classified as ghostlore, we can't have a witness, or a bunch of witnesses. Once a witness enters the scene, ghostlore shifts to something else—call it an anomalous event, or a ghost encounter, or a tale of the unexplained. In this book, several stories do feature a real witness, or a bunch of real witnesses, who say they experienced something—often at sites that are the focus of railroad ghostlore, but not always—for which they could not find a natural explanation. Could they be mistaken, or discounting some natural occurrence that might explain the activity? Could they just be pulling a prank? Could they be trying to create their own haunted railroad legends?

Absolutely.

But, there's always this remarkable little phrase, "what if," when you're dealing with these sorts of stories: the brushes with the liminal regions of our consciousness between the real and the fake, the natural and the supernatural, death and life.

What if there are more to these stories of railroad ghosts and spirits? What if some—maybe even a small percentage—are more than simply grassroots fables and practical jokes? What if emotionally charged events, like the technological shock of seeing steam- and diesel-driven machines and witnessing the tragedy of horrific railroad accidents, can embed themselves into the space and time of the epicenter of these occurrences? What if the industry that helped change our consciousness from a world of farms and pastures into a world of factories and industry, and led to what some researchers phrased the annihilation of space and time, also altered our consciousness in such a way that it allows us to probe into deeper dimensions of reality?

Those are difficult questions—questions, maybe, that we can never answer. And that might be a good thing.

NOTES AND SOURCES

Chapter 1

Abraham Lincoln Ghost Train

Black, Andrew. "The Lincoln Ghost Train." *Mask of Reason* (blog). https://maskofreason.wordpress.com/the-book-of-mysteries/eerie-ohio/the-lincoln-ghost-train/.

Goodheart, Adam. "How Abraham Lincoln's Funeral Train Journey Made History." *National Geographic*, April 18, 2015. https://news.nationalgeographic.com/2015/04/150418-abraham-lincoln-funeral-train-railroad-civil-war-history/.

Lamkin, Virginia. "Lincoln's Phantom Train." *Seeks Ghosts* (blog), November 4, 2014. https://seeksghosts.blogspot.com/2014/11/lincolns-phantom-train.html.

Nosowitz, Dann. "The Strange History and Future of Lincoln's Funeral Train." Atlas Obscura, April 14, 2015. https://www.atlasobscura.com/articles/the-strange-history-and-future-of-lincoln-s-funeral-train.

Selzer, Adam. *Ghosts of Lincoln: Discovering His Paranormal Legacy*. Woodbury, MN: Llewellyn, 2015. p. 193–224.

Rebel Ghost Train Rises Again

Jacobs, Jack. "Ghost light legend haunts King William railroad crossing." *Virginia Gazette,* October 25, 2017. http://www.vagazette.com/va-vg-tr-ghost-light-1025-story.html.

"The Light at Cohoke Crossing - King William County." The Haunted Commonwealth. May 20, 2010. http://hauntedva.blogspot.com/2010/05/light-at-cohoke-crossing-king-william.html.

Bravehaunts: The Ghost Trains of Scotland

Adams, Paul. *Little Book of Ghosts*. Gloucestershire, UK: The History Press, 2014. p. 136–157.

"The Tay Bridge Disaster." Haunted Scotland Investigates. August 22, 2013. http://haunted-scotland.co.uk/the-tay-bridge-disaster/.

Holder, Geoff. *Haunted Dundee*. Gloucestershire, UK: The History Press, 2012. p. 75–76.

"Haunted Locations." Must See Scotland. https://must-see-scotland.com/haunted-locations/.

Rannachan, Tom. *Psychic Scotland: A Journey to the Other Side of Scotland*. Edinburgh, UK: Black & White Publishing, 2007.

"Ghost Trains of Great Britain." Strange Days. October 23, 2007. http://www.strangedayz.co.uk/2007/10/ghost-trains-of-great-britain.html.

A Time-Traveling Ghost Train?

"Fairytale or Fact: The Wales 'Spectral Train' Mystery." Phantoms and Monsters. December 10, 2015. https://www.phantomsandmonsters.com/2015/12/fairytale-or-fact-wales-spectral-train.html.

Ghost Train of the Santa Ana

"Anaheim to Santa Ana." Abandoned Rails. http://www.abandonedrails.com/Anaheim_to_Santa_Ana.

"Your Nightmares Were True: The Ghost Train on the Abandoned Tracks in Santa Ana." Backpackerverse. https://backpackerverse.com/abandoned-train-santa-ana/.

Do Famous Sci-Fi Writers Dream of Locomotive Spirits?

Dick, Anne. *The Search for Philip K. Dick*. San Francisco, California: Tachyon Publications, 1995. p. 62.

Ely, Nicole. "Marin's Haunted History." Patch, October 31, 2012. https://patch.com/california/sanrafael/marin-s-haunted-history.

"The Engineer's Revenge." *Fairweather Lewis* (blog). October 6, 2012. https://fairweatherlewis.wordpress.com/2012/10/06/the-engineers-revenge/.

Ghost Train or Eerie Railroad Premonition?

"The Phantom Train of Medicine Hat." Hammerson Peters. http://hammersonpeters.com/?p=725.

Schlosser, S. E. "Ghost Train: An Alberta Ghost Story." American Folklore. http://americanfolklore.net/folklore/2010/07/ghost_train.html.

Scary Scandinavian Ghost Train

Grundhauser, Eric. "The Silver Arrow, the Real Ghost Train Haunting the Stockholm Metro." Atlas Obscura, October 07, 2015. https://www.atlasobscura.com/articles/the-silver-arrow-the-real-ghost-train-haunting-the-stockholm-metro.

Schneider, Kate. "The ghost train that haunted Stockholm." News.com.au. https://www.news.com.au/travel/travel-ideas/weird-and-wacky/the-ghost-train-that-haunted-stockholm/news-story/c3c550bf0d53aef2ba9efa60646c39ab.

Chapter 2

"Haunted Cabooses." *Journal of the Bizarre* (blog). March 31, 2018. http://web.archive.org/web/20180417102330/http://www.journalofthebizarre.com/2018/03/haunted-cabooses.html.

The Canyon Motel. http://thecanyonmotel.com/williams_az_motel_caboose_rooms_suites.html.

Jameson S. "Haunted Lake County: Featherbed Inn." YouTube video, 7:15, May 23, 2017. https://www.youtube.com/watch?v=AoSeDz8NI-o.

Chapter 3

The Railroaders Memorial Museum

"Altoona Railroad Museum Documents Ghost Hauntings in Altoona." Pennsylvania Mountains of Attractions. http://www.pennsylvania-mountains-of-attractions.com/ghost.html.

Railroaders Memorial Museum. https://www.railroadcity.com/.

Also based on personal interviews with ghost hunters of JABA Paranormal.

Has a Haunted Hobo Boarded a Railroad Museum Without a Pass?

Cusumano, Katherine. "10 Supposedly Haunted Museums." Mental Floss, October 29, 2015. http://mentalfloss.com/article/70356/10-supposedly-haunted-museums.

Mad River Museum. http://www.madrivermuseum.org/about.html.

Martin, Douglas. "Steam Train Maury, 5-Time Hobo King, Is Dead at 89." *New York Times,* November 23, 2006. http://www.nytimes.com/2006/11/23/us/23graham.html.

"Railroad Museum to Host Paranormal Investigation." Shop Bellevue Ohio. September 26, 2014. http://www.shopbellevueohio.com/information/blog/item/railroad-museum-to-host-paranormal-investigation.

Waves of Paranormal Phenomena

Cousins, Blake. "Third Phase of the Moon." YouTube video, 5:33, October 31, 2011. https://www.youtube.com/watch?v=gMycEjY5Xb4.

Haunted Earth Ghost Videos (blog). April 3, 2012. http://hauntedearthghostvideos.blogspot.com/2012/04/hcrc-is-video-sent-to-me-by-poster.html.

"History of Hawaii Consolidated Railroad—Laupahoehoe Train Museum." Laupahoehoe Train Museum. http://www.thetrainmuseum.com/history.html.

Of History, Heritage, and Hauntings

Brunswick Heritage Museum. http://brunswickmuseum.org/.

"Haunted Brunswick Maryland: Frederick County/Brunswick Heritage Museum Ghost Expedition 2017." *Maryland Paranormal Research* (blog). http://blog.maryland-paranormal.com/post/59830542767/haunted-brunswick-maryland-frederick-county.

Maryland Paranormal Research. "Brunswick Heritage Museum Ghost Expedition 2017/Frederick County ('Dave')." YouTube video, 1:20, October 22, 2017. https://www.youtube.com/watch?v=p4FQqbXshsE.

Mason Dixon Ghost Hunters. http://www.masondixonghosthunters.com/.

"Maryland Museum Haunted by Ghosts?" NBC Washington. https://www.nbcwashington.com/news/local/Maryland-Museum-Haunted-By-Ghosts-97792664.html.

National Railroad Museum Features a Five-Star Haunting

"Investigations." Fox Valley Ghost Hunters. http://www.fvghosthunters.com/investigations/.

McMahon, Todd. "Railroad museum expansion on long-distance track." *Green Bay Gazette*, August 10, 2016. https://www.greenbaypressgazette.com/story/news/local/2016/08/10/museum-expansion-long-distance-track/88421872/.

Midwestern Paranormal Investigative Network. "National Railroad Museum—Green Bay, WI." https://mpinetwork.wordpress.com/mpininvestigations/national-railroad-museum-green-bay-wi/.

Georgia State Railroad Museum

"Most Haunted Places in America: Roundhouse Railroad Museum." Ghosteyes. http://web.archive.org/.web/20110514114137/

http://www.ghosteyes.com/haunts-roundhouse-railroad-museum.
"Georgia State Railroad Museum." Savannah. http://www.savannah.com/the-roundhouse-railroad-museum/.
"Savannah Roundhouse Railroad Museum." Trolley Tours. https://www.trolleytours.com/savannah/roundhouse-railroad-museum.

Restless Spirits in the Sleeping Quarters

Gallagher, Margaret. "Is the Port Moody Station Museum haunted?" *CBC*. October 31, 2016. http://www.cbc.ca/news/canada/british-columbia/is-the-port-moody-station-museum-haunted-1.3828869.
Northern Paranormal Investigations. http://www.northernparanormalinvestigations.ca/welcome.html.
"Haunting at the Museum?" Port Moody Museum. April 4, 2010. http://portmoodymuseum.org/2010/04/09/haunting-at-the-museum/.

Chapter 4

Was a Weird Specter Seen at a Train Yard Sent to Warn Workers, Residents?

Keel, John. *The Mothman Prophecies*. Avondale Estates, GA: IlluMiNet Press, 1991.
"Mothman." Roadside America. https://www.roadsideamerica.com/story/12036.
"The Man in Black: The Mystery of Pennsylvania's Flood Visitor, a Spooky Stranger that Predicted Disaster." Week in Weird. January 1, 2014. http://weekinweird.com/2014/01/30/the-man-in-black-pennsylvanias-flood-visitor/.

Civil War Spirits Haunt Gettysburg Engine House

Ghost Adventures. "Gettysburg." Season 4, Episode 1. Aired September 17, 2010. Daily Motion. http://www.dailymotion.com/video/xqhiur_ghost-adventures-gettysburg_shortfilms.

Nesbitt, Mark. *Civil War Ghost Trails: Stories from America's Most Haunted Battlefields*. Mechanicsburg, Pennsylvania: Stackpole Books, 2012. p. 97–106.

Clschauer. "Ghosts of Gettysburg—The Engine House." YouTube video, 2:53, November 13, 2008. https://www.youtube.com/watch?v=0yMK_wZYrtk.

Tracking Ogden's Historic Railroad Past and Its Haunted Present

DeVoy, Beverly. "Many a Ghost Haunts Ogden, According to Area Legends." *Deseret News*. October 28, 1991. https://www.deseretnews.com/article/190629/MANY-A-GHOST-HAUNTS-OGDEN-ACCORDING-TO-AREA-LEGENDS.html.

Free, Cathy. "Cathy Free: Friends seek out ghostly haunts." *Deseret News*. October 27, 2010. https://www.deseretnews.com/article/700076879/Friends-seek-out-ghostly-haunts.html.

Jones, Jennifer. "The Death Trunk of Haunted Union Station." The Dead History, January 18, 2016. https://www.thedeadhistory.com/haunted-utah/death-trunk-union-station/.

———. "Frank Yentzer: The Ghost of Ogden's Union Station." The Dead History, February 19, 2013. https://www.thedeadhistory.com/haunted-utah/frank-yentzer-ghost-ogdens-union-station/.

———. *Ghosts of Ogden, Brigham City and Logan*. Charleston, SC: History Press, 2017.

The chapter is also based on personal email correspondences between Jennifer Jones and the author.

Ghosts on the Waterfront

Christensen, Jo-Anne. *Ghost Stories of British Columbia*. Toronto: Hounslow Press, 2000. p. 95.

Daily Hive. "The Most Haunted Building in Vancouver: Waterfront Station." October 31, 2012. http://dailyhive.com/vancouver/haunted-vancouver-waterfront-station.

Sutherland, Joel. *Haunted Canada 6: More Terrifying True Stories*. Toronto: Scholastic Canada, 2016. p. 36–40.

Tubes of Terror: The UK's Supernatural Subway System

Barnicoat, Becky. "9 Creepy-As-Hell London Underground Ghost Stories." Buzzfeed, May 22, 2017. https://www.buzzfeed.com/beckybarnicoat/incredibly-creepy-stories-about-the-london-underground?utm_term=.piVMjWBr9L#.cown4a1Vzv.

"Bethnal Green Underground Tube Station, London Underground Ghosts." Haunted Rooms. https://www.hauntedrooms.co.uk/bethnal-green-underground-tube-station-london.

Strunck, Clara. "Spotting a GHOST on the tube might make you think twice about your commute." *Daily Star,* June 2, 2016. https://www.dailystar.co.uk/news/weird-news/520156/Ghost-spotted-London-underground-tube-viral-video.

"5 Most Haunted London Underground Stations." Top 5s. June 11, 2018. https://www.top5s.co.uk/5-most-haunted-london-underground-stations/.

Union Station and the Ghost of Abigail

"Ghosts at Union Station Hotel." Ghost Village. http://www.ghostvillage.com/encounters/2008/02042008.shtml.

Lombard, Cherish. "Room 711 at Union Station is permanently occupied." WKRN, October 26, 2017. http://www.wkrn.com/special-reports/haunted-tennessee/room-711-at-union-station-is-permanently-occupied/1077055802.

Chapter 5

The Haunted Horseshoe Curve

"The Legend of the Horseshoe Curve Tunnel." *Discovery PA* (blog). October 3, 2014. http://discoverypa.blogspot.com/2014/10/the-legend-of-horseshoe-curve-tunnel.html.

Colin Kurtz. "3 Guys Go Ghost Hunting in the Horseshoe Curve Tunnel, Altoona, PA." YouTube video, 9:29, October 17, 2016. https://www.youtube.com/watch?v=RVQXSq8S7No&t=1s.

Tunnel of Terror— Sensabaugh Tunnel's Dark Past May Shed Light on Its Current Paranormal Popularity

KPR Crew. "Legends of Sensabaugh Tunnel." https://kprcrew.com/portfolio/legends-of-sensabaugh-tunnel/.

Knox Paranormal Researchers. "Baby Crying EVP in Sensabaugh Tunnel." YouTube video, 0:17, March 16, 2015. https://www.youtube.com/watch?v=MewiDRFwKUM.

Additional Source: Police Report # 0370300, Mount Carmel, Tennessee.

Flinderation and the Supernatural Railroad Nation

Anderson, Michael. "Paranormal Investigation and Flinderation Tunnel." Ghosts and Stories. https://ghostsandstories.com/paranormal-investigation-at-flinderation-tunnel.html.

Flinderation Tunnel photos. Facebook. https://www.facebook.com/pg/Flinderation-Tunnel-144572778961793/photos/?tab=album&album_id=144573035628434.

"Flinderation Tunnel." *Haunts and History* (blog). https://web.archive.org/web/20140521235058/hauntsandhistory.blogspot.com/2011/11/flinderation-tunnel.html.

Chapter 6

Eerie Echoes—The Return of the Red Arrow

Altoona Mirror. "Locals Tell Story of the Red Arrow 70 Years After Railroad Disaster." February 17, 2017. Accessed December 13, 2017. http://www.altoonamirror.com/news/local-news/2017/02/locals-tell-story-of-the-red-arrow-70-years-after-railroad-disaster/.

"Altoona, Pennsylvania Ghost Sightings." Ghosts of America. http://www.ghostsofamerica.com/1/Pennsylvania_Altoona_ghost_sightings2.html.

Nesbitt, Mark and Patty A. Wilson. *The Big Book of Pennsylvania Ghost Stories*. Mechanicsburg, PA: Stackpole Books, 2008. p. 150–152.

McIlnay, Dennis. *The Wreck of the Red Arrow: An American Train Tragedy*. Hollidaysburg, PA: Seven Oaks Press, 2010.

"The Wreck of the Red Arrow." *Patty Wilson* (blog). September 22, 2011. Accessed December 12, 2017. http://patty-wilson.blogspot.com/2011/09/wreck-of-red-arrow.html.

Dead Railroad Men Do Tell Tales

"Malvern." Haunted Places. http://hauntednorthamerica.net/all-locations-listing/all-locations-usa-ne/malvern/.

"Restless Spirits at Duffy's Cut." Phantoms and Monsters. July 13, 2017. https://www.phantomsandmonsters.com/2017/07/restless-spirits-at-duffys-cut.html.

"Seeking the Ghosts of Duffy's Cut." Phantoms and Monsters. August 20, 2010. http://www.phantomsandmonsters.com/2010/08/seeking-ghosts-of-duffys-cut.html.

Rafferty, Meghan. "Grandfather's ghost story leads to mysterious mass grave." CNN, August 24, 2010. http://www.cnn.com/2010/CRIME/08/24/pennsylvania.graves.mystery/index.html.

"The Haunting at Duffy's Cut." *Seeks Ghost* (blog). May 12, 2013. https://seeksghosts.blogspot.com/2013/05/the-haunting-at-duffys-cut.html.

The Legends of America's Most Haunted Railroad Crossing

"Chilling Tales of Haunted San Antonio." *Express News*. October 29, 2017. https://www.expressnews.com/sa300/article/Chilling-tales-of-haunted-San-Antonio-12314236.php.

"The Legend of the Haunted Railroad Tracks." Ghost City Tours. https://ghostcitytours.com/san-antonio/haunted-places/haunted-railroad-tracks/.

Spirit Photography Captures Eerie Signs of Haunted Railroad History

"Dickenson Level Rail Crossing." Hamilton Paranormal. http://hamiltonparanormal.com/railtrail1.html.

"The Haunting of the Sydenham Rd. Rail Bridge, Dundas, Ontario." Hamilton Paranormal. February 8, 2003. http://hamiltonparanormal.com/bridge10.html.

The Case of the Chatsworth Disaster and the Glowing Grave

"The Chatsworth Disaster: The haunted history of Illinois' worst train disaster." American Hauntings. https://www.americanhauntingsink.com/chatsworth/.

Harper's Weekly. "The Illinois Railroad Accident." August 20, 1887. http://www.catskillarchive.com/rrextra/wkill.html.

The Screaming Bridge

Criscuolo, Nina. "Avon's Haunted Bridge: The Truth Behind the Tales." WISH TV, October 27, 2017. http://www.wishtv.com/news/local-news/avons-haunted-bridge-the-truth-behind-the-tales_2018040306543654/1096489973.

"Avon's Haunted Bridge." Town of Avon official. http://www.avongov.org/egov/documents/1446048459_62506.pdf.

Chapter 7

Railroad Ghost Story Gets Presidential Seal of Approval

Burke, James C. "The Legend of Joe Baldwin." Wilmington Railroad Museum. http://www.wrrm.org/the-legend-of-joe-baldwin.html.

"The Maco Light." North Carolina Ghosts. https://northcarolinaghosts.com/coast/maco-light/.

Preik, Brooks Newton. *Haunted Wilmington.* Wilmington, North Carolina: Banks Channel Books, 1995. p. 23–28.

Steelman, Ben. "Brunswick's 'True' Ghost Story." *The Star News.* https://www.starnewsonline.com/news/20081010/the-maco-light-brunswicks-true-ghost-story.

The Paulding Light

"Paulding Light." Atlas Obscura. https://www.atlasobscura.com/places/paulding-light.

Goodrich, Marcia. "Just in Time for Halloween: Michigan Tech Students Solve the Mystery of the Paulding Light." Michigan Tech news, October 28, 2010. http://www.mtu.edu/news/stories/2010/october/just-time-for-halloween-michigan-tech-students-solve-mystery-paulding-light.html.

"The Paulding Light." The Paulding Light. November 25, 2013. http://www.pauldinglight.com/.

A Spectral Brakeman Who Never Takes a Break

Kelemen, Ed. *Pennsylvania's Haunted Railroads.* New Florence, PA: Nemelke Publishing, 2018.

1888 Ghost Rider of the Rails

Clark, Jerome. *Unnatural Phenomena: A Guide to the Bizarre Wonders of North America.* Santa Barbara, CA: ABC-CLIO, 2005. p. 357.

A Not-So-Thankful Thanksgiving Day Haunting

Jones, Jennifer. "The Thanksgiving Ghost." The Dead History. November 23, 2017. Accessed January 28, 2018. https://www.thedeadhistory.com/haunted-america/thanksgiving-ghost/.

Also based on personal email communications between Jones and the author.

He May Have Died at His Station but He Left a Restless Spirit

Clark, Jerome. *Unnatural Phenomena: A Guide to the Bizarre Wonders of North America*. Santa Barbara, CA: ABC-CLIO, 2005. p. 110.

"Brition S. Craft." Find A Grave. https://www.findagrave.com/memorial/54352579/brition-s-craft.

KMBC 9. "Ghost Stories: Atchison Railroad Legend." YouTube video, 2:52, October 31, 2008. https://www.youtube.com/watch?v=GIHgopiGBFk.

The Natural State Boasts Some Supernatural Railroad Tales

"Things to Do—Haunted Arkansas." Arkansas. https://www.arkansas.com/things-to-do/uniquely-arkansas/haunted-arkansas/mysterious-lights/.

"A mysterious light floating in the trees of Gurdon, Arkansas may be a piezoelectric effect." Atlas Obscura. https://www.atlasobscura.com/places/gurdon-light.

"Crossett Light." Encyclopedia of Arkansas. March 7, 2011. https://www.tripsavvy.com/gurdon-light-2211874.

Galiana, Amanda. Trip Savvy, July 29, 2017. https://www.tripsavvy.com/gurdon-light-2211874.

Taylor, Troy. "Haunted Arkansas—The Gurdon Light." Prairie Ghosts. http://www.prairieghosts.com/gurdon.html.

Northern Spook Light: Canada's Famous Railway Ghost Light

"10 Strange Unsolved Train Mysteries." *North Atlantic* (blog). September 5, 2017. https://northatlanticblog.wordpress.com/2017/09/05/ghost-train-the-st-louis-light/.

Riemer, Taryn. "Ghost Train Story Haunts Small Saskatchewan Community." *The Western Producer.* https://www.producer.com/2014/10/ghost-train-story-haunts-small-saskatchewan-community/.

The Suitor House: Canada's Spirit Weigh Station

Bell, David. "These could be the spookiest spots in Calgary's most 'haunted' neighbourhood." *CBC News*, October 31, 2017. https://www.cbc.ca/news/canada/calgary/calgary-ghost-haunted-house-inglewood-johanna-lane-1.4380114.

"Suitor House." Paranormal Studies & Inquiry Canada. http://psican.org/index.php/ghosts-a-hauntings/alberta/391-the-suitor-house.

Dead Worker's Ghost Gives Whole New Meaning to Being "Fired"

"Dead Workman's Apparition." *Phantoms and Monsters* (blog). September 9, 2016. https://www.phantomsandmonsters.com/2016/09/dead-workmans-apparition.html?.

Conclusion

Schivelbusch, Wolfgang. "Railroad Space and Railroad Time." *New German Critique* 14 (Spring 1978): 31–40. https://www.jstor.org/stable/i221171.

To Write to the Author

If you wish to contact the author or would like more information about this book, please write to the author in care of Llewellyn Worldwide Ltd. and we will forward your request. Both the author and publisher appreciate hearing from you and learning of your enjoyment of this book and how it has helped you. Llewellyn Worldwide Ltd. cannot guarantee that every letter written to the author can be answered, but all will be forwarded. Please write to:

Matthew L. Swayne
℅ Llewellyn Worldwide
2143 Wooddale Drive
Woodbury, MN 55125-2989

Please enclose a self-addressed stamped envelope for reply, or $1.00 to cover costs. If outside the U.S.A., enclose an international postal reply coupon.

Many of Llewellyn's authors have websites with additional information and resources. For more information, please visit our website at http://www.llewellyn.com